Woking Library
0300 2010 1001

11/10

$e$

v-2010

SURREY
COUNTY COUNCIL

Overdue items may incur charges
as published in the current
Schedule of Charges.

L21

Matador
5 Weir Road
Kibworth Beauchamp
Leicester LE8 0LQ, UK
Tel: 0116 279 2299
Fax: 0116 279 2277
Email: books@troubador.co.uk
Web: www.troubador.co.uk/matador

ISBN 978 184876-516-0

British Library Cataloguing in Publication Data.
A catalogue record for this book is available from the British Library.

Typeset in 11pt Sabon by Troubador Publishing Ltd, Leicester, UK
Printed in the UK by TJ International Ltd, Padstow, Cornwall

**Matador** is an imprint of Troubador Publishing Ltd

*To my mother, a true and very splendid rose*
*And to my daughter, a chip off the old rose block*

# CONTENTS

# THE ROSE

*Some say love, is like a river that drowns the tender reed.*
*Some say love, is like a razor that leaves your soul to bleed.*
*Some say love is like a hunger an endless aching need. God*
*says love, is like a flower, and you its special seed.*

*But the heart afraid of breaking will never learn to dance.*
*The dream afraid of waking will never take the chance. Are*
*you the one who won't be taken, who cannot seem to give,*
*and the soul afraid of dying, that never learns to live?*

*When the night has been too lonely and the road has been*
*too long, and you think that love is only for the lucky and*
*the strong, just remember in the winter, far beneath the*
*bitter snows, lies the seed that with the Son's love, in the*
*spring becomes the Rose.*

Bette Midler (Adapted)

The Son himself was called The Rose of Sharon. In his
love we will see and know love. The Son himself says
"Woman thou art loosed." Are you free to receive life
and to blossom? Are you free to be the rose?

A woman who is a rose is a woman who is free,

loosed from the bondage of the ideas of what men and women think she can or can't do, free to be herself and fulfil her true potential as God intended for her.

I found myself perplexed as a growing young girl by what I began to perceive as the ideas of others about what I should be. I had the support of good parents, an enlightened and forward thinking father and a mother who was the first female pharmacist of her tribe, the Ibos, and I could afford to ignore the pressures to conform to the ideas of others and be myself but as I grew older I was faced with many issues which I had to tackle myself and take decisions which had far reaching meaning for my life. Of all the constraints that men and women sought to place upon me the most perplexing was that I could not serve God in any way I wanted, I could not preach, not allowed, some well meaning men and women told me. I could not pray with my head unveiled, I could not do this, I could not do that.

I decided that I had to search the scriptures for myself on this topic and, in prayer, I allowed the Holy Spirit to lead me by the hand and teach me from the word of God. Much as I loved Jehovah, I did not want my love for God himself to cause me to disobey God by taking on that which he did not want me to take on and thereby doing that which was outside his will. I was delighted to find that as I had suspected, God placed no constraints on women. I was established and liberated by this and I knew that I was loosed from the chains of false constraints and condemnation forever. "Woman thou art loosed," the Lord said to a woman healed of deformity. That is how I felt as I was loosed from any worry that I might have the wrong end of the stick.

In the Bible, in the course of my study, I found different types of women, women like me, women very different from me. But there was one thing they all had in common and that is this. THERE IS NO LIMIT TO WHAT GOD WILL DO WITH ANY LIFE THAT IS FULLY SURRENDERED TO HIS WILL. I found strong women, apparently insignificant women, women who were very good, women who were bad, leaders, housewives, beauties, not so beautiful, judges, warriors, prostitutes, women who had children, women who did not have children, queens, slaves, happily married, unhappily married. I found them all. One woman only had a baby. Guess what, He became Saviour of the World.

There is a blueprint for the life of each of us which is planned for us by God himself (Ephesians 2:10). These plans were made for our lives even before we were born (Jeremiah 1:3). Happiness and freedom lie in finding that blueprint and walking in it. Never mind other people and their quest for their life's blueprint, seek God's will for your life and walk in it. There is no point competing with the Joneses. If you must compete, compete with yourself to be the best you that God intended, but first you must find out what that is. A clear understanding of this basic attitude to life is a great antidote against jealousy and envy. If you have the best for yourself why seek what someone else has?

The study which led me to the writing of this book brought me great peace of mind. I have always known from the great upbringing of loving parents that I can be whoever I want to be and do whatever I want to do to make the best of my life but society and at many levels even other Christians told me differently.

Instinctively I knew that God could not have consigned a whole sex to powerlessness and inferiority so I decided to search the scriptures for myself. Guided by the Holy Spirit I confirmed the truth that was in my heart. Yes there are many problems in the attitude of many people to women, even in the Church, but I am glad, so glad to tell you all that it is their problem, not one ordained by God the Father, Son and Holy Spirit.

It is my hope and prayer that as you read this book, you will also hear the voice of Jesus in your life saying "Woman thou art loosed." It is my hope that in reading this book, you will clarify in the Lord who you are and that you will rise up, go to your destiny and walk in it

I do not know your name but God does. Your name may be Susan or Jane or Tracey or Sharon, you may be Chioma or Sola or Jamilla or Zainab, you may be Genina or Hella or Ingrid or Bjork, whatever your name is, remember that a rose by any other name will be as sweet.

# WOMEN WHO OPERATED AT GOVERNMENTAL LEVEL

## DEBORAH

Judges Chapters 4 and 5
*"The inhabitants of the villages ceased, they ceased in Israel, until I Deborah arose,.....arose as a mother in Israel."*
*Judges 5:7*

Under the palm tree she sat judging Israel. She was the spiritual and temporal head of Israel. The story is simple enough. God spoke to her in the course of her duties as Judge and Prophet and asked her to send for Barak and muster the armies of Israel to fight Sisera King of Canaan who at the time was a source of constant threat to her people. God had spoken to Barak but Barak had simply persuaded himself that he was not hearing right because the task was too great.

In those days, Israel had no king. Their spiritual leaders were also their temporal leaders. After Moses, there had been Joshua and other Judges. Then Deborah became a Judge. I have never heard any sermons about this woman other than the ones I have preached. No one talks about her. She bucks the trend and does not fit the teaching that women are spiritually limited in what they can do even from those who grudgingly accept that we can in fact be secular leaders but not spiritual leaders. So it would seem that according to some we can be Judges and Prime Ministers and get to any level of temporal government but we cannot be leaders in the Church. Well according to the Bible from which we take our authority for everything, she was a spiritual and temporal leader of the people of God. So many people argue that Jesus did not have women amongst the Apostles. Neither did he have gentiles but which one of us is going to argue that only Jewish men can be priests. We will look at the overall position of Jesus with regard to women when we look at Women in the Ministry of Jesus and we will see that, not only did he not limit women but he clearly honoured them with the greatest spiritual responsibilities.

Deborah was a woman who had so fulfilled her calling that when she called, everyone answered. She is an example for us all. Whatever we have to do, it is our duty to do it well and our reputation will speak for us. When she called to Barak and all Israel, they answered. She was consistent and reliable. She kept appointments and kept time. Whenever you needed Deborah, she was there. That is why all Israel came up to her for judgement. If she had not been reliable they would not have come.

When I have asked some male preachers about Deborah, they have said she was only a Judge when the men of Israel were all cowards. In other words it was not originally God's will for her to be a temporal or spiritual leader but she was picked because no man would answer. Rubbish. The text does not say that. In any event, on another occasion when Israel lived in fear and all the men had turned into cowards, God still chose a male coward and made a courageous warrior out of him. His name was Gideon. No I am persuaded that God intended to call Deborah as spiritual and temporal head in Israel and did so. She was no substitute for any failed man. In fact one of the messages of the Book of Judges is that God used all kinds of people from different walks of life for this supreme post. Ehud the left handed was a bit of an odd ball, Gideon was a coward, to start with anyway and Deborah was a woman. They were all different types of people.

Deborah was the daughter of Ephraim. Ephraim and Manasseh were the sons of Joseph. Joseph was a leader in Egypt and it is a sad fact but even in those days, the people of the world were often more advanced in accepting women for who they were than the people of God. Joseph clearly accepted that liberated view of women which the Egyptians had at the time even to the extent of having women Pharaohs. Joseph's children and great grand children would have carried on the tradition and attitudes in which they were brought up (See Sheerah). Deborah came from a family and lineage from which she learned how to respect herself, how not to limit herself. Had that not been so, how would she have known that God was calling her to take on the mantle of temporal and spiritual leader of the nation?

Today governments struggle to take on the role assigned to families whilst the importance of the family is being derogated. All their attempts at social engineering fail because they are seeking to take on roles which are not theirs. Parents and families, beware, you cannot abrogate your responsibility to your children. God has created us in families and put within that structure the potential to impact a child's life. If you want the best for your children, teach your children the way that they should go and when they grow up they will not forget it.

For Christian women, indeed all women, it is important to note that for all that she was in the land, for all her status, spiritual and temporal, Deborah was known as the wife of Lappidoth. At no time did she start wearing the pants in the home. At no time did she allow the status of her husband to be diminished. At no time did she allow their relationship to suffer nor did she insist on being known any differently. Some of today's women would consider it an affront if they were known as the wife of their husband but Deborah was secure in herself enough to know that was an honour and part of her exemplary life. A woman who competes with her husband just does not get it and vice versa. The two have become one. What he does and who he is, is to her glory and what she does and who she is, is to his glory. A man needs to be honoured and respected by his wife and whether we like it or not, there are certain roles that are important and part of a man's image of himself. I have watched marriages fall apart where a professional woman or working woman has left the husband in the home and gone out to work whilst he becomes a full time house husband. This role pattern does not last long. More often than not the relationship will deteriorate and there will be a divorce. Men are different from women. We are really not exactly the same. The fight of misguided women libbers has been to make us all the same. The fight of any enlightened Christian is for each person man or woman to be free in Christ to fulfil their God given potential not for war of the sexes.

Deborah was a prayerful woman. Only those who are steeped in prayer can hear God on a consistent basis. It is worth noting that the oppression under which the children of Israel lived at the time had gone on for twenty years. How long did Deborah pray for Israel and lead the children of God in prayer? What could Israel do against Jabin, his commander Sisera, their weapons of warfare and their nine hundred chariots of iron? Deborah did not lose heart. She knew how to wait for the promise of God and how to persist in prayer till she got her answer. Though the promise tarry, we must wait for it. It will surely come. That vision does not lie. The promise of God shall surely be fulfilled. He is Jehovah Jireh, El Shaddai, El-Elohim, omniscient, omnipresent, the Almighty God. We must learn patience and faith as Deborah had in abundance.

In prayer she heard the Lord's directions and sent for Barak and the sons of Naphtali and Zebulum and said to them,

"Thus says the Lord "Go and march to Mount Tabor and take with you ten thousand men from your tribes. I will draw out to you Sisera, the commander of Jabin's army with his chariots and his many troops to the river Kishon and I will give him into your hand."

Although this was a just war, a war of self-defence after years of oppression, it is worth noting that when God was ready to deal with Sisera, the children of Israel did not remain in the cowards' position. They were asked to move on the enemy not wait till the enemy was upon them as before. They marched towards the enemy with the promise of God. We are not meant to walk in fear. Even when we are afraid, we must walk forward in faith. Deborah knew this because she lived it and she heard it directly from God. She had a sure-safe battle plan because she had received it from God.

Barak showed his cowardly side. He did not want to go to battle without the strength of this remarkable woman beside him.

"I will not go if you will not go with me." he said

"I will surely go with you. But because of the way you are going about it, God will give the honour of this battle to a woman." Deborah replied. She did not mean herself as we will discover in due course. There was another, a woman for whom the glory of that particular war was destined.

She did not berate him for being a coward but was determined instead to help him, to build him up, to bring out the best in him. So, good women do. Good women do not emasculate, nag, abuse or put down even when deserved. Lay emphasis on the good in people, not the bad in them if you want to build them up. She did not pretend the bad was not there, just knew how to turn a coward into a great general, leading by example and encouraging when necessary.

As far as I can see, it was the Lord's plan to complete the honour and confidence he had in this woman by making her a joint leader with Barak of the armies of Israel against a terrible foe such as Jabin's army. She was definitely meant to go to war. The only thing that changed was that the honour of killing Sisera was not going to go to Barak the Commander in Chief of the Army but to a woman.

We therefore see that within the will of God as far back as the Iron Age a woman of God was a spiritual leader, a temporal leader and a Commander in Chief of the Army of her people. Boadicea of the Iceni was not an aberration. She too lived as spiritual and temporal leader of the Iceni and as Commander in Chief of her army.

Deborah's power was not a physical power. Deborah's power was spiritual. She relied entirely on God. She was bound to win. Women are physically not as strong as men and it is no use pretending that we are or seeking to be. That is not how we are made. But that does not limit us in what we can do. However it is important to note that Deborah did not seek physical combat with any man. There is no record of that. In our freedom to be who God wants us to be, we should always know our limitations. It would have been foolish of her to take on a physical challenge that a physically stronger man could do better. She did not seek to do so because she was not trying to prove anything. She was secure in who she was, a woman of God.

All those years ago, her husband trusted her to go off with a whole army of men and in close quarters to her co-commander in Chief, Barak. What if she went off with one of the soldiers? That was never a fear. In all the years that she had with Lappidoth during which she came to be known as the wife of Lappidoth, they had built such trust in their marriage that they had no fear of or for each other. Such marriages are meant to be. There is a freedom that comes when there is true trust and this Deborah clearly had.

There are some women called into the Ministry

whose husbands are not called into the Ministry. There are some women called into the Ministry who are not married at all. It is important that such women identify within themselves that they are thoroughly within the will of God. Those who choose not to understand their situation have a problem which they will hopefully solve for themselves by going to the scriptures but it is worth noting that there is certainly a problem out there. Some people will be moved to pray when they see a husband and wife team where the wife is called into the ministry and the husband is not, so that the husband can take over and the wife can relax, whatever that means. Such prayers are misguided and without insight. But one should not be dented by such things. Know who you are and move on in the power and grace of God.

The glory of killing Sisera did go to a woman, another woman that we shall meet in a later chapter. It is important however to note that when Deborah sang the song of victory, she remembered this woman. She did not have problems about giving praise to another woman. Women are so often unkind to one another and some find it hard to acknowledge the gifting and ability of other women. When you are secure in your own place in God, the security of another woman of their own place in God can only be a source of praise to God and not a source for competition or challenge, however subtle. Sisters, let us grow up and praise God for one another and for his grace to each one. Let us support where we can and God in turn will support us as He always does.

Deborah continued to pray. Her battle plan came from the Lord. She knew the time, she knew the hour for attack and Barak trusted her too. He was a good man and knew how to recognise a woman of God and to trust her. When Deborah said,

"Arise. This is the day to finish off Sisera because the Lord has gone before you," Barak had no doubt.

And finish Sisera's army he did, he and his army. But he did not kill Sisera. Deborah had said the honour would go to a woman and she did not lie. Deborah never lied or exaggerated. She was faithful and true.

Deborah praised all the participants of the war but the true glory went to God. All true spiritual leaders know this, that of ourselves we can do nothing. It is "not by might nor by power but by my Spirit" says the Lord. Immediately victory was assured, that same day the glory went to God as Deborah and Barak led the songs of praise and thanksgiving.

It is worth noting that when David killed Goliath, the women of Israel sang in praise of David but when Deborah the woman of God sang, the glory went to God although she praised all participants too. She taught Barak also to sing to God. In her song she also praised her fellow warriors and Jael whose role is contained in another chapter. She did not forget herself out of some false sense of modesty. She thanked God for what he had used her to do, causing her to arise to help her people. But she thanked God mostly because she had remained herself and remained true to her sex whatever her achievements. She thanked God that she had arisen not as a man, not as a father but as a MOTHER IN ISRAEL.

# MIRIAM

*"For I brought thee up out of the land of Egypt, and
redeemed thee out of the house of servants, and I sent
before thee Moses, Aaron, and Miriam" Micah 6:4
Exodus Chapter 1 and 2, Numbers Chapter 12*

Moses led the children of Israel from Egypt to the
outskirts of Canaan. He had two helpers that he
himself had appointed. One was his half brother Aaron
and the other was his big sister Miriam. In Exodus
15:20 we see that Miriam was a prophetess. In the
above passage, it says quite clearly that she was a
leader in Israel appointed not just by her brother but
by God.

She was obviously old enough to plot and be of
use to her mother when Moses was born. He was born
at one of the darkest times in the history of the
Hebrews. The Hebrews had become slaves and the
people who had enslaved them had forgotten all that
they were to each other and their shared history and
had become oppressive to them, using them as
disposable slaves. The people around them hated them
so much that they had started a genocide programme
against these immigrant slaves. But God was with the
immigrant slaves as God often is with the underdog
undergoing undue suffering. Miriam was resilient and
innovative and refused to be just a victim. When her
mother was pregnant she must have been well aware
that she could not keep her baby, if it was a boy and
Miriam worked on a plan with her mother. It is quite

possible that this plan came directly from Miriam herself as she prayed and sought the Lord for the safety of her newborn sibling. It was an amazing plan, one that could only have come from revelation and the throne of a God with a sense of humour. The throne of Egypt was to care for and bring up the one who was going to lead the children of Israel out of Egyptian slavery!

When Moses was born, it is clear that Miriam went beyond the call of duty. She risked her own life to ensure the safety of Moses, constrained by nothing but the love of her new born brother and possibly some awareness of the specialness of this baby in the sight of God. She had knowledge even at a young age of the ins and outs of the city. She obviously knew where Pharaoh's daughter went to bathe with her maidens of honour. When she and her mother laid the baby Moses in the crib of bulrushes, she kept watch over him, bearing her own discomfort like the little trooper that she was, committed to staying the course however long it took. She was present and alert, no doubt praying when the right time came. As soon as Pharaoh's daughter who had no children of her own saw the baby she knew she had to have him. Miriam was there on hand to jump out and offer a nurse for the baby. The nurse? Their mother, of course, and so Moses the ultimate arch enemy of Egypt was brought up by his own mother inside the palace of the very people who had not only enslaved them but put out a partial genocide edict on the lives of their tribesmen by ordering that all their male babies should be killed. So, purposed Jehovah.

And so Moses had the best education in the palace,

the best training, the best food and facilities. But he also had the best spiritual training. His mother and Miriam were obviously regular visitors to the Palace, at least in his early years and in those years they managed to teach him everything he needed to know about Jehovah the great God of the Hebrews and the whole world. With the prophetic gifts of Miriam she must have known and taught Moses something of his own destiny. That is probably why Moses killed the Egyptian who was troubling a Hebrew. He was young then and had not yet learned that the ways of Jehovah are not human ways.

When he did learn and succeeded in the first part of his mission, at the beginning of the journey, he appointed Miriam and Aaron as co-leaders of Israel.

I would like to say that Miriam was a perfect leader. She was a great sister but her love for her brother did sometimes get in the way. Sometimes we can become selfish in love. There is no evidence that she married and had her own family and unfortunately this left her open to interfere with her brother's family and she overstepped the mark. In Numbers we are told that Moses had married a Cushite. Zipporah was a Cushite and their children were of mixed race. Cushites were Southern Saharan inhabitants, Africans. Zipporah was a black African woman and she was married to Moses all those years ago! These are things that you will rarely hear from the pulpit. Miriam was not sensible with her and joined in the murmurs against her, possibly on account of her race. Her father Jethro is described as the Priest of Midian. He was clearly a believer and not only did he take care of Moses when he was a fugitive, but he came to see him when he brought his wife back to him and gave him good counsel. Moses clearly had the greatest of respect for this great man and took his counsel to great benefit for himself and his people. But Miriam was jealous, probably of not being the main female in the life of Moses anymore, possibly because she was being racist. The Lord did not tolerate that and the Bible says that Miriam was struck with leprosy albeit for a short time to teach her a lesson. Please do not get me wrong, I do not say that sickness is always a result of sin or is always punishment, but in this instance the Bible says that it was. Miriam did not freely and graciously give way to Zipporah and allow her new sister-in-law to manage her husband's household. Her mother had probably died by this time and she was effectively being a nightmare as the interfering mother in law / maiden sister. But the Lord taught her to let go, the hard way.

Here is a lesson for us all. It is a serious thing to interfere in a family however we do it, whatever our justification. Mothers in law, maiden aunts, spinster sisters beware. Allow your new sister-in-law, daughter-in-law to take charge of their own home. That way everyone will be so much happier. That is the way that God intended it. Therefore shall a man leave his father and his mother and cleave unto his wife and the two shall become one flesh. The family is the most important unit in human organisation for the well being and happiness of man. It was as God made it in the beginning. We ignore the sacred principles to our cost. Show me a broken society anywhere and I will show you disrespect for marriage and an inordinate amount of marriage breakdowns.

The significance of Miriam is that she was a leader in Israel from the beginning. She was operating at government level and apart from the spat with her sister-in-law, there is no evidence that she ever put a foot wrong again.

Was Miriam chosen because she was Moses' sister and because someone had to be there to represent the women? No. Moses did everything in accordance with the pattern which God showed him. Moses did everything on God's direction. Miriam was a leader in Israel because God chose her to be so and it says so quite clearly in the book of Micah the prophet. So right at the beginning of the history of the people of God, God himself chose a woman amongst their leaders. When God himself visited Abraham through his Angels to announce to him that he was to be the father of many nations he also had his Angels speak to Sarah. Abram's name became Abraham and Sarai became Sarah (Genesis 17:15-19). God has never left the women out. He has never left them behind in leadership stakes.

# THE FIVE DAUGHTERS OF ZALOPHEHAD

*"So the Lord blessed the latter years of Job more than his beginning.......In all the land were no women found so fair as the daughters of Job and their father gave them inheritance among their brethren."*
*Job 42:12-15, Numbers 27 1-12*

Miriam was not the only woman who made headlines in those days. A group of five sisters lost their father in the wilderness. When the Israelites were within sight of the Canaan, Moses began to look at the partitioning of the land. All the men were lined up for apportionment. The five daughters of Zalophehad watched this for a while and decided to go to Moses to ask for their portion so they went up to Moses and said,

"Our father died in the wilderness but we are here. We may not be boys but we are his children. We want our portion thank you very much."

Moses was a godly and respectful man. The civilisation of the Court of Egypt where women became Pharaohs equally as the men had rubbed off on him. His closeness to the living God had completed the process and as a result he treated everyone with due respect. He did not dismiss them outright. He decided to pray about this matter and enquire of the Lord, as always. The Lord's reply is interesting. He did not just say, yes you can give them their portion. He said,

"The daughters of Zalophehad are right. Give them their portion."

What a liberating thought that these five women with the men were amongst the original inheritors of the land of Canaan. They were simple ordinary girls who knew God in their hearts and knew that they were valued and honoured by God. They were clearly secure in their upbringing and knew that they had value like everyone else. They came forward and changed the law and traditions of men. Today as we struggle with parliamentary domination and find our governments passing laws that are not to our liking or do not comply with our faith, we can come forward in pressure groups or individually through talking and writing to our MPs, writing to newspapers and doing what we can to support the work of major pressure groups that take stands that we agree with, in prayer and giving. Joanna Lumley and her campaign on behalf of the Gurkhas has become legendary. Anyone can change things that need changing. Yes we can.

There is no record that any other women got their portion at that time, although many had lost their fathers in the wilderness. Only those who had the gumption to believe in themselves and kick against wrongful mindsets and traditions got their portion. Those who refused to come forward, who risked nothing, lost out. These girls could have become the disgruntled pariahs of their people by stepping forward the way they did but they did so with courage and confidence discerning the heart of God. What they did however did not just benefit them, but created a general recognition that girls in similar situations could potentially inherit land.

Job, a man who had been through a terrible experience that brought him face to face with God, literally, gave landed inheritance to his daughters Keziah, Jemimah and Keren amongst their brothers. I find that men of God who have really experienced God generally do not have any problems with women being themselves and rising to any level of leadership inside or outside the Church and having possession rights that men have. It is those who have tied themselves in religious knots and refuse to know and understand the heart of God and their fellow human beings who are a problem.

"For in him there is neither Jew nor Greek, there is neither bond nor free, there is neither male nor female, for you are all one in Christ Jesus." Galatians 3:28

This particular story offers great support to Christians in third world countries and other parts of the world where women do not traditionally inherit property or land. If God almighty says that the daughters of Zalophehad are right, then we must have the courage to live in accordance with God's values not man's values.

It is advisable and sensible for Christians to make a will because when they have gone to be with the Lord, their loved ones including their females will have a clear written document of their wishes. In most countries, but by no means all, the courts and traditional authorities will honour the will of a deceased person. At the very least it will give the female relatives some basis for stating their case and it is more likely than not that the Courts and traditionalists will give some honour to the will of a deceased loved one.

# SHEBA

*2 Chronicles 9*
*1 Kings 10*
*"And when the Queen of Sheba heard of the fame of Solomon concerning the name of the Lord, she came to prove him with hard questions."*

*I Kings 10:9*

She did not only operate at government level, she was the government.

The Queen of Sheba came from Ethiopia. There is no doubt that she was real and that she was Queen over a large part of sub Saharan Africa, in history.

Her story is set out in the book of Chronicles and in the book of Kings but it is the Kings' version that I prefer for one simple reason. It explains more fully why she came to see King Solomon. She had heard of his wealth and fame and wisdom but it was not just that. It was his wisdom CONCERNING THE NAME OF THE LORD. Sheba had heard from her merchants about this famous King who believed in one God. She had worked it out. His beliefs had to have something to do with his greatness, success and wisdom. She wanted the best for her kingdom. She wanted to learn but most of all I believe it was her need for the one God that drew her to make the great journey by camel wagon train to the kingdom of Solomon.

She was not mistaken. She found all that she was looking for. King Solomon did not disappoint but herein lies the significance of Sheba. She was a woman who was great enough to put her new God Jehovah, her people and their need to hear about the new God and her duties, before personal happiness. What a fine example she is to all our modern day philosophies and attitudes that say we must put ourselves and our own happiness first at all times. But truly the people who are great are the people who follow the example of the life of the Master, King Jesus and put others before themselves. No one says we should not care about ourselves at all but we have become too selfish and self centred in modern thinking. To love our neighbours as ourselves, we must love ourselves too but modern life demands too much of personal pleasure and too much of oneself above all else. These days it is even said that parents should not have to make sacrifices for their children and it is implied or even said that it is wrong to do so. How can any child know that they are loved and cherished above all else if they are not put before anything that the parents want? Even for the rich the way we allocate our time will say a lot to our children and spouses even if money is no object. Love is something you do, not just something you say or feel.

Sheba and Solomon fell in love. There is little doubt that the Song of Songs was written by Solomon about their love affair. It would appear that despite his three hundred concubines and seven hundred wives, he had room for one more. From the Song of Songs it is clear that theirs was a particularly passionate and heady relationship. The object of the song is described in clear terms,

"Dark am I yet lovely,
O daughters of Jerusalem dark like the tents of Kedar
Like the tent curtains of Solomon
Do not stare at me because I am dark
My mother's sons were angry with me
and made me take care of the vineyard"
*Song of Songs reputed to be by King Solomon*

Her hair is described as being like a flock of goats descending from Mount Gilead. There is much reference to myrrh which was a great export of Ethiopia in those days and remains so to this day. There are many other references in the book that make it clear that Sheba was the object and inspiration of this great love. She must have had that serene brand of female beauty that only Ethiopian and Somalian women seem to have. For the beauty of Sheba think David Bowie's wife, Iman and even beyond. Let us put it this way, Solomon was too old a fish to be caught with a bent hook. With all those wives and concubines, she had to be something else and she was.

How many women today will give up such a heady affair to do the right thing? How many women today knowing that they had wealth and passion unlimited would give it all up for the sake of duty. Sheba did because her focus was not herself but the reason why she came originally constrained her. She had come to see King Solomon and to enquire after his wisdom concerning the name of the LORD. She had found her Lord and her duty was to take the good news of the one true God, the God of love, the creator God, the almighty God back to her own people. She gave all up for the sake of doing the right thing before

Jehovah and that is exactly what made this woman and all the other women in this book great. First they knew who they were and what their gifts were and what God wanted of them and secondly, they wasted no time doing it, because they put their God before everything else and put their trust in him.

In the ancient tales of the white man's first forays into Africa, they tell of a Christian kingdom in the middle of the African continent. No one understood how this mystery came to be, that in the middle of the African continent there was a Christian kingdom that was well run and well advanced in architecture and trade. There were no records of any previous forays of Europeans into Africa and yet there was this advanced Christian kingdom. It was a mystery that the historians and legend writers such as Rider Haggard and John Buchan were unable to solve. But they and others spoke of this kingdom as did Marco Polo and other well known explorers. Those who read the Bible knew the answer. It was indeed the case that no Europeans had been into the heartland of Africa before the first known forays of the 15th century but those who read the Bible knew that the Christian kingdom was not only real but owed its existence to the journey of a great Queen who went on an epic journey to see a great King to find out about his wisdom concerning the name of the Lord. Her name was Sheba and she returned to her people to teach them first about the existence of the great God Jehovah and about the ways of the people of Jehovah.

Every year from that first visit, key members of the royal household of Ethiopia travelled unfailingly to

Jerusalem for the Passover feast. They kept this tradition going for a few hundred years.

When Jesus ascended into heaven after his crucifixion he handed the responsibility of building the Church to his apostles and disciples. Those who were steadfast became the first Ministers of the Church. They were filled with the Holy Spirit on the day of Pentecost and began to evangelise. On the first day of Pentecost three thousand people were added to the Church. A few days later following the healing at the Beautiful Gate another two thousand were added to the Church. Daily the believers bore witness to Christ and grew in number until the persecution and murder of Stephen. This led to the dispersal of Christians from Jerusalem. The good thing about this is that the Christians gave up their comfortable niche in Jerusalem and began to spread even to the uttermost parts of the earth even as the Lord intended them to and commanded them to.

It is a remarkable thing that the first recorded person in Acts of the Apostles to hear the gospel of Jesus Christ was an African from the Court of the Queen of Sheba! The Ethiopian Eunuch had come for Passover as they of the royal household had done over the centuries from the time of Sheba's visit and conversion. On his way back he was still reading his Old Testament as he clearly often did. Acts Chapter 8 tells us how the Holy Spirit told Philip to get into the carriage with the Eunuch and explain to him what he was reading about. As it happened he was reading about the Prophet's account of the death and resurrection of Christ and its meaning which although contained in the passage was not immediately clear to whoever read it and it eluded him as it did anyone who did not yet understand the truth about Jesus. Philip was able to show him how it related to Christ and the things that were being talked about in Jerusalem during that period. The eunuch believed and was baptised. What grace to the great Queen of the South. For centuries the fire that was set in her heart which she in turn passed on to her own people did not die. They completely honoured God and God completely honoured them.

Today less is made of this story than God intended. Jesus himself said that the Queen of the South will rise in judgement against the children of this generation. She went to see Solomon concerning the name of the Lord and yet a far greater one than Solomon was with them. The obscurity of the Ethiopian Church today has not always been so. John Buchan wrote a book entitled "Prester John." Prester John simply means John the Priest. John was in fact a descendant of the Queen of Sheba and Solomon. When the great Queen left Judea she was pregnant with Solomon's baby. She could so easily have stayed for her own sake and for her child's sake but she gave up all that because she knew she was the only person who could take back the knowledge of the true God to her people and be accepted. She knew she had been away long enough and they needed her for their survival.

Prester John built a chapel in Jerusalem which is in existence till this day. The interaction between Jerusalem and Ethiopia remained for centuries and even till this day many Ethiopians speak Amharic the special brand of the Hebrew language which Christ spoke along with Aramaic. Indeed as far back as

Moses, the priest of Midian, Moses' father in law was said to be a Cushite, an Ethiopian. The reference is in the book of Numbers 12:1 which says quite clearly that Moses married an Ethiopian woman. In the history of Moses, when he fled from Egypt he had found refuge with the Priest of Midian Jethro and had married his daughter Zipporah. There is clear reference to the fact that Moses not only lived with his father in law before the exodus but also spent time with him whilst he and the children of Israel were nomads in the desert looking for the land of Canaan. He received very good advice from the Ethiopian and clearly treated him with great respect.

But few refer to the significant role of this black man and his family and other black men of greatness in the Bible just as few refer to the greatness of women in the annals of this great Book, the Bible.

Sheba's child was given the title which was promised to a descendant of Solomon. Till this day one of the titles of the Ethiopian kings is "Lion of the tribe of Judah". Haile Selassie who was an Ethiopian King had this title. When he went to Jamaica in the nineteen fifties, descending from the skies in a white airplane, wearing his well known white military uniform, the Jamaicans could not believe that such pomp and ceremony belonged to Africa. Africa following slavery was to them the continent of darkness. When they heard that his title was "Lion of the tribe of Judah" some cannabis sozzled ones amongst the Jamaican people thought that this meant that the Christ was an African. Haile Sellasie quickly became their godhead as the Christ that was to be born of the Royal line of David and Ethiopia and

Abyssinia the promised land. This as a matter of interest is the origins of rastafarianism, as a group of disenfranchised black people sought a spiritual and temporal identity.

But the Church founded by Sheba and more specifically the Ethiopian Eunuch thrived and lives till his day. Some say that Sheba's son was given the Ark of the Covenant to mind. It is indeed a fact that the Ark is no longer in Zion, but as the events of the end times unfold, it is believed that the Ark will be found and returned to Israel. It may well be that it is in Ethiopia guarded by the sacred priests of the Ethiopian Coptic Church. Some claim that this is so.

# ESTHER

*"A thing of beauty is a joy forever*
*Its loveliness increases; it will never pass into nothingness*
*But still will keep, a bower quiet for us*
*And a sleep full of sweet dreams, and health, and quiet*
*breathing"*
*John Keats – Ode to Beauty*

### The Book of Esther

She walks in beauty but beauty has many faces. In the case of Esther beauty was true. In the case of Vashti who also features in her story beauty was not so true. The beauty of women is often seen as something destructive, manipulative, and evil. This is just plain daft. If God creates someone with physical beauty, how can that be a bad thing? In Esther's case it clearly was not. Yes, beauty can be used to captivate, to manipulate and to destroy but that is a personal choice, not the result of beauty. When beauty is godly, we have godly results, when beauty is ungodly, we have ungodly results. There were other beautiful women in the Bible, Jezebel, Delilah, Herodias. They worshipped pagan Gods and behaved in pagan ways. Their beauty became bywords for evil but Esther worshipped Jehovah from whom all goodness flow and she remains the epitome of what a truly beautiful woman is and can be, beautiful inside and outside.

Esther was an immigrant. In fact she was less than that because her people had not voluntarily migrated to Susa. They had been conquered and brought in as spoils of war. She certainly had very few rights in the community in which she lived. Her parents were dead and only her Uncle Mordecai looked after her. He was a god-fearing man and brought up the young Esther in the ways of God. Well does Proverbs say, "Teach a child the way that he should go and when he grows up he will not forget it." Both they and Mordecai her guardian Uncle did just that and Esther never forgot the things she had been brought up to believe.

When an edict of the king went out it was clear what was to happen. There was to be a beauty competition, in effect and the most beautiful would marry the King. I wonder how many Christian women today would enter a beauty competition. Would we not say it is of the world forgetting that we are called to be in the world but not of the world. Of course it matters very much what the ultimate aim of the competition is. In this case, to marry a King. That cannot be bad in itself. Christians reject so many things these days and will not be involved in things that are crying out for our presence. We are now suffering for it because other people have taken key places in the nation and in the world and are now calling the shots in a direct opposition in many cases to Christianity. School boards need us, hospital boards need us, the professions, government and indeed every area of life other than those involved in direct evil. Who knows but that you may have been born for such a time as this? Who knows what difference you might make?

When Esther entered the palace, she got on well with everyone. She immediately won the favour of Hegai to whom she was entrusted. Esther was given the best beauty treatments and special healthy food. She was given the best places and female attendants.

Esther did not initially reveal her nationality and background but simply got on with everyone. Some immigrants wear their nationality like a badge of unfriendliness, refusing to mix with the people of the land to which God had chosen to bring them, refusing to change and adapt and mix and when they are rejected, they become upset. Yes of course, racism is real but a lot of people out there are good people willing to live and let live. I personally believe that if one comes to live in another's country, one can honour that country by adapting as much as one can to that country. Whilst we all have a lot to learn from people of other races and cultures, multiculturalism as preached by present day politicians at its worst can result in confusion, as indeed it did during the attempt to build the Tower of Babel in ancient Babylon.

The favour Esther had did not go to her head. She never presumed to know better than Hegai to whom she had been entrusted. She did use well chosen creams and ointments to enhance her beauty and this might provide an answer to those who are worried about cosmetics. I would say choose wisely and with good information but do your best to keep and even enhance the beauty that God has given you. It is part of his gift to you. When it was time for her to go to the King, she had the good sense to rely entirely on Hegai's advice as to what to wear and how to apply her make up and perfumes. She was no prima donna, nor did her instant popularity go to her head. As a result she listened to the advice of the expert and the final result was stunning. Her beauty fully enhanced, she had no trouble pleasing the King who chose her as his wife. She won the beauty competition and got the prize, a King!

When Esther became Queen she was still who she always was. Nothing went to her head. Mordecai could still get to her and he did very soon with a plot he had uncovered, the very genocide of the Jews. More than that, although Esther was not wearing her nationality like a badge but simply getting on with the people amongst whom she lived first as a sub-proletariat and then as their Queen, at no time did she compromise her religion. Inside the palace she started the quiet work of witnessing and she built a prayer group around her of ladies in waiting who worshipped the true God and prayed with their Queen. In fact it was not just Mordecai who kept in touch with Esther but she with him as well. It was she who sent her servants to find out what was wrong with Mordecai as he had become distraught by news of the plan of genocide. Esther was in touch enough to notice and having noticed made enquiries.

When Esther heard the news she made a great resolve. She would go to the King without first being summoned by the King. "If I die, I die, but I will go." She was determined to go to the King and ask him to do that which had never been done before, to overrule his own law which had already been passed. The edict for genocide had already been signed. To ask for it to be unsigned would have meant her own death unless she succeeded. She called her palace prayer group to prayer and made an edict for all the Jews to fast and pray with her. She did not rely on her beauty or the physical attraction that the King had for her. This woman was wise and had more respect for her King than that. He was not a shallow man who could be swayed by the superficial. She knew that she needed the power of God to get him to change his mind.

She succeeded because her power was in her God not in herself. Her beauty was only a part of who she was. Her real motivation and source was Jehovah. And he cannot lose.

As for Harman the very gallows he had built for the people of God saw his own death. God used a woman of great beauty to turn the tables on the devil.

The feast that Esther called in celebration of the deliverance of the Jews from genocide is still honoured to this day. It is called the feast of Purim celebrated by all Jews from the days of Esther to the present day. One young but truly beautiful woman was prepared to risk her life to prevent the genocide of her people and her great dedication and courage has never and can never be forgotten.

I have never understood how with the example of the woman Esther many preachers still rail at us from the pulpit about the evil of women. Delilah and Jezebel take up so much space. I have little to say about them except to say that they were beautiful women too but the difference between them and Esther is that Esther served the living God and they served the demon gods. The evil in them flowed from who they served and the goodness in Esther flowed from her service of the good and living God.

Esther's husband King Xerxes had a first wife that Esther replaced. The difference between the two women is worth noting. There is no doubt that Vashti even if she wanted to do anything in similar circumstances to Esther would have relied only on her beauty and from a strong and dutiful king would have received nothing but scorn and probable loss of her own life. The reality of Vashti is that she belittled her husband. How many of us have done this or belittled other men by refusing to show them respect? The man was the King for goodness sake but Vashti refused him the appropriate respect. Everyone wants respect. It is a natural and deep seated need. One of the things that has struck me about gangs today is that most of their motivation comes from the need for "Respec'". No one can force love which is our ultimate desire but respect is simply one human being acknowledging the humanity of another human being and is within us to give to everyone. We all need love but no one can force that. Respect however is a matter of choice and we are very foolish when we deny others their due respect. This always has consequences as it is deeply upsetting.

When the King threw a party he was proud of Vashti's beauty and sent for her to show her off but Vashti showed him up instead. What was wrong with her? Why could she not just graciously accept his pride in her beauty. It did not mean that he thought she was just a pretty face and even if he did, why not just deal with it calmly and then discuss it later with him. Sometimes we are too harsh on our men picking at their faults whether real or imagined and then the things that we pay attention to begin to loom larger and larger till they are out of proportion through our own condemnation. We should learn to be sweet to our men, to forgive their imperfections up to a point and to lay emphasis on their good points.

Vashti competed with her husband instead of

enhancing him and taking pride in who he was. She threw her own party when he threw his. What a foolish woman. She could have had a party any other time and concentrated on what she could do to make her King and husband's party more successful but oh no it had to be competition time. What a foolish girl.

I mentioned three women Jezebel, Delilah and Herodias. Jezebel was the wife of King Ahab. She was a very beautiful woman and used her beauty to mesmerise the King. She was also very crafty and whatever the King wanted, the King got. Jezebel would see to it. She did not speak about right and wrong. She was a plotter and a murderess and an inciter several times over. The story of what she did to Naboth to get his vineyard and family inheritance for the King is chilling. She incited men in her pay who made false accusations against Naboth and stoned him to death. She brought in her own religion and persecuted those serious with their Jewish faith, causing all the prophets of God to go into hiding or become compromisers. She hounded in particular the most powerful prophet of them all, the prophet Elijah who would neither hide in fear nor compromise. She did not stop the worshiping of Jehovah directly, just made it very clear that if you worshipped her demon gods you ate at the King's table and if you did not, well best hide in a cave or what happened to Naboth would happen to you; trumped up charges and death by stoning. She struck fear into the heart of the bravest. Some people argue that she was not sexually promiscuous but she was. When Jehu managed to clean up the nation and become King, one of Jezebel's last acts was to try to turn him into her toy boy. She was pushed like a broken rag doll from the top of her chambers by her guardian eunuch at the instigation of Jehu. She died on the spot.

Delilah was married to Judge Samson but her heart was with her own people and their pagan worship so she deceived her husband, found out his source of strength and betrayed him. This eventually resulted in his capture, suffering and death so palpably portrayed by John Milton in his epic Samson Agonistes.

Herodias was the wife of one of the Tetrarch ruler brothers during the time of Jesus and John the Baptist. She was a slut. What else would you call a woman who not only had an affair with her brother in law, openly and shamelessly, but used her daughter and her hypnotic pagan dance to bring about the death of John the Baptist. To ask for the head of a holy man on a platter is indeed macabre. But these three women have often been used by men to degrade women by giving us their qualities and attitudes. We can only share their kind of behaviour when we share their gods. None of these women worshipped the Judaeo-Christian God. They worshipped demon pagan gods. When modern women behave like them, who do they worship? There is nothing dignifying for women to emulate in the person of these three girls or their lives.

In the story of Esther, we have some examples of the clear difference between the modern day women libbers and the type of godly liberation of women of which I speak. Vashti may not have felt like going to show herself off to all those drunken leering men at the party, but she should have known that could not have been what her husband meant when he asked for her to come to the party in her glory. It was clearly his pride in her that he wanted to display but she saw it the wrong way. She reacted the wrong way and destroyed her marriage for no good reason. She misread him and over-reacted without any consideration as to how she was making him look before the whole world. If she thought about it, she did not care. How could she be his wife? Of course he could have forgiven her but I am speaking to women here and someone must show good sense when it is going wrong. If your marriage is important to you and it should be, wisdom, patience, forgiveness and most of all goodness and godliness will help to save it. What is the secret of a good marriage? The answer is in the question. Goodness.

# (EXTRA)ORDINARY AND (IN)SIGNIFICANT WOMEN

## JAEL

*"Blessed are they that mourn for they shall be comforted*
*Blessed are the meek for they shall inherit the earth"*
*Jesus – Sermon on the Mount Matthew 5:4-5*


*Judges Chapter 4 and 5*

When Deborah and Barak defeated the armies of Sisera and Jabin, the prophetess had given a specific prophecy about how the war was to end. The glory was Jehovah's of course, but in human terms, she had said through prescience that the glory of the victory of the war would not go to Barak but to a woman. Had she meant herself, she would have said so. In her song of battle she had sung about herself as well as Barak and about the other soldiers who participated in the great battle. No, Deborah meant someone else, someone unknown and obscure whose name had she stated it would have meant nothing to anyone who heard it. Deborah sang about Jael, the insignificant woman who smote Sisera with a tent peg.

Deep in the vales of Zaanannim near Kedesh amongst the tents of the settlers was the tent of Jael the wife of Heber the Kenite who had left the other Kenites the descendants of Hobah, Moses brother in law. Heber had broken ranks with his own people who were closely associated through Zipporah and her father to the Israelites. He was effectively a saboteur to his own people and associated with the enemies of Israel. How else would Sisera think that he would be safe in the tent of Jael and Heber?

Jael is a great example of an ordinary woman who had no influence whatsoever with her husband. She clearly did not approve of the new association between her husband and the enemy of the Jewish people, but she kept her mouth shut and kept a watchful eye on things.

Her opportunity came when Sisera, on the run from the battle front, made for her tent believing he was going to a place of safety, a welcome place. He reckoned without understanding what Jehovah meant to those who love him. Jael's husband had defected spiritually but not she.

She served him poisoned milk so that he went to sleep. When he was asleep she took a tent peg and stuck it through the frontal lobe of his head. And so Sisera the great war general of Canaan finally died and the war was over. Beware, all who enter Jael's tents who are enemies of Jehovah. Thus shall they perish.

This woman never fails to amaze me. She was an apparently powerless woman. She did her daily chores of putting up the tents and minding the house and fetching and cooking and serving her husband and his guests. She had no influence over him but she kept her own counsel. Her husband was not on God's side but she remained in her marriage guarding her home and keeping herself on God's side. What an example for many women whose husbands may not be Christians or may be lukewarm Christians. You stay married, you stay faithful and strong and you stay prayerful and watchful and when the enemy enters your home, you see him off in prayer or actions, whatever it takes.

It is often the case that it is women who see danger to their home before men do. I can spot a lady who has designs on my husband of thirty five years long before he ever can. Fortunately I can talk to him about this and he, bless him, will take necessary precautions. I can see other danger in the family before he can, quite often. This is not strange. Right from Genesis, the beginning, the Lord has put special enmity between the devil and woman (Gen 3:15) when the prophecy was given that a man born of woman will bruise the serpent's head. Just as Jael did to Sisera, a man born of woman will destroy the devil. This prophecy looks forward from the beginning to the birth of Christ but the point here also is that women are given special sensitivity to detect evil especially in their home. That is why God said to Abraham "listen to your wife." (Genesis 21:12 ). Despite the great mistake that Sarah made in giving her servant to her husband to fulfil God's promise of a child (as if God needs help) it was not her mistake that God concentrated on but all the goodness and support that she had given Abraham all those years in the wilderness.

God's gift to women to discern evil especially in the home is so very important these days. Jael did not say "I had better wait till Heber comes home. He will know what to do or I can talk him into what to do." She knew that if she did that, she would be made to cook Sisera the choicest lamb stew and keep him safe. She saw her chance and took it. It could not have been easy for that little woman to drive a shrapnel of wood into the head of another human being but she did what she had to do. She knew that if she did not kill him more of the Jewish people and others would continue to be killed. So she steeled her little heart to granite and did that which some think that only a man could do. She could not invite him to a sword fight or use her own physical strength against him. She used her wisdom to devise a way to deal with the enemy of her home and of her people.

Today we call on all housewives, sisters, mothers and all women connected to the home to keep a good look out for this haunt of the enemy. The home is God's creation on earth for the happiness and security of all of us, where we can experience something of the wonderful love of Jehovah for mankind. No wonder the devil fights so hard to destroy families. Show me any broken society and I will show you broken homes and broken dreams, an inordinate amount of them. But ladies instead of demanding that we behave like our men, let us rather, in devotion to God keep spiritual watch over our homes seeing off any Sisera or any other evil that seeks to attack. We do not have to talk too much; prayer, including spiritual warfare, wisdom and the right action at the right time will often do the trick.

The action of Jael, one little woman, proved an inspiration to others. We are told that the Israelites knowing that Sisera was dead grew stronger and stronger till they subdued Jabin the Canaan King and destroyed him.

# THE LITTLE MAID

*By the rivers of Babylon*
*There we sat down*
*Yea we wept*
*When we remembered Zion*
*When the wicked*
*Carried us away to captivity*
*Required from us a song,*
*Now how can we sing the Lord's song*
*In a strange land*

Boney-M

*2 Kings Chapter 5*

She captures my imagination, this lonely sad little girl, or was she? No, she should have been sad and lonely but it is clear that even at such a tender age and with no spiritual support around her, she managed to push away the sadness and loneliness and live.

The little Jewish maid was a captive from one of the many wars between the Jews and the Syrians. She must have been of noble Jewish birth because a lot of the noble captives like Daniel and his friends Shadrach, Mishak and Abadnego were sent either into the royal household of the captors or into the home of high officials. What a dreadful thing it must have been for this child who was so slight that she was called the little maid to be removed from her comfortable home, her parents and her friends to a place unknown where she was no longer waited on but had to wait on a mistress. Bitterness, anger and self-pity would have been the only way to go but the little maid despite her young age and with no one to encourage her chose not to go that way. At such a young age she had learned in whatever condition she was to be thankful. She had learned that neither life nor death nor angels nor anything in the world could separate her from the love of God. You see she had been brought up to know Jehovah and to worship him with all her little heart. And she did. There is no doubt that despite her young age, she walked in the prophetic. How else would she know what her mistress's husband had to do to get well. There were no medical curative powers in the waters of the river Jordan. She may have guessed but I think it was more than that.

God did not desert the little girl in her captivity. He gave her a kind mistress, the wife of Naaman. They would talk together and laugh together. Naaman's wife must have become a kind of surrogate mother to her. God never deserts us. The psalmist said, "though I walk in the valley of the shadow of death, thou art with me." God allows suffering but if we continue to be faithful to God even the most appalling things can have some good come of them. Whatever happens, God will do something to show that he is God and that he is with you. In the case of Joseph whilst in prison for something he did not do (attempted rape when he was the victim of sexual harassment and abuse) God used his gift of interpretation of dreams to mark out a bearable niche for him in the prison dungeons. In the case of the little maid, God gave her loving little heart a mother figure.

She could have prayed against the family of her

captors. They were the enemy who had destroyed her whole nation. She did not. She prayed for their good, even as the Lord had prayed from the cross "Father forgive them for they know not what they do." It was whilst praying for them that she heard from God in a prophetic way. She realised that God wanted to heal Naaman and she plucked up the courage to go and tell her mistress that her husband should go and see the prophet Elisha in Samaria.

Naaman must have suffered for years and despite every attempt to keep his disease a secret as was always the case with leprosy in those days, his suffering must have been so great that his loving wife had to tell the little maid. She must have been observant enough to notice, in any event and concerned enough to ask about her Master because she cared. When she was told, she went on her knees. This little child who could have been praying for hell and damnation on her captors and masters prayed for the healing of this man instead.

Naaman was not nice unlike his wife. When the courageous little girl went to him to tell him what God had said, there seemed to be no word of thanks. She asked him to find the prophet Elisha but Naaman wrote to the King instead. What could the King do? How like the human way of thinking to believe that earthly status goes hand in hand with spiritual status. The King had as much clue what to do as a fly. Fortunately for Naaman, the prophet Elisha eventually heard of it and decided to help this man.

"Go and bathe in the River Jordan seven times and you will be healed," the prophet told Naaman.

But Naaman's response was sheer uncouth arrogance.

"How dare you think your country is anything compared to mine? You are a nobody preacher man and so are the rest of your people. Have we not rivers in my country greater than all the rivers of your country put together. Go away preacher man."

The little maid cared enough not to go away. Somehow she broke through the walls of his fear which masqueraded as arrogance and she got him to go to the Jordan. Naaman eventually humbled himself and went in obedience to the Lord God and came back clean.

Nothing more was heard of the little maid. Like Dickens' Little Dorrit, she continued about her business living her life the best she could, thankful for whatever came her way and knowing that the best way to fight despair is to fill one's heart with the goodness of Jehovah. As Paul said to the Phillipians in 4:8,

"Let your gentleness be known to all. The Lord is near. Do not be anxious about anything but in everything by prayer and petition with thanksgiving let your requests be known to God. And the peace of God which passes all understanding will keep your hearts and minds in Christ Jesus. Finally brethren whatsoever is true, whatsoever is noble, whatsoever is right, whatsoever is pure, whatsoever is lovely, whatsoever is admirable, whatsoever is of good report, if anything is praiseworthy and admirable think about those things. Whatsoever you have received from me, think about these things."

The only way out of well deserved depression (where circumstances really are dire and sustained) is the way of the little maid. She was likely never to see her parents again even if they were alive. Everything she knew was gone, friends, home, neighbours, brothers and sisters, parents, all gone. She should have been depressed but she guarded her heart and thought instead of good things, her friendship with her new mother figure, her new home and the fact that she could be of help to others even if only in prayer and a word of advice. Her secret, she remained faithful to her God and the teachings of her God. No wonder whenever she knocked in prayer on the doors of heaven, it opened and she got real and specific answers.

# THE BUILDING SITE LABOURERS

*Go to the ant you sluggard and learn of it*
*Consider her ways and be wise*
*Which having no guide overseer or ruler*
*Provideth her meat in the summer*
*And gathereth her food in the harvest*

Proverb 6:6-8

*Nehemiah Chapter 3*

There is something very macho about the building site. Many men with fat bellies and trousers that hardly fit, think that from behind the steel helmets and the dust covered faces, and the safety of this male preserve, they can shout out anonymously to women as they walk past. Not every builder does this, of course, but it happens. Well I have news for them, the building trade is not a preserve for men. It might be work better suited for men because of the lifting of heavy material involved but it is not a male preserve. If that is what you as a woman want to do, go ahead and do it!

The daughters of Shallum were labouring builders along with all the Jewish remnant left after the captivity and destruction of Jerusalem. This is the sacking of Jerusalem which led to the captivity of Esther. During that period, Nehemiah had also been captured and like so many of these God fearing Jews, had found favour in the sight of the captors, as in the case of Nehemiah and Esther and Daniel and many others at Royal level. The King himself had not only given Nehemiah permission to go and rebuild the very walls which his armies had torn down, so great was the impact of this god-fearing man on the King, but he had also given him materials and finance for the rebuilding of the wall of Jerusalem.

Nehemiah had been able to cautiously persuade the remnant to come out as a people and work together to achieve such a huge task, the re-building of the wall of Jerusalem.

Shallum was the only one who brought his daughters with him. But then he was an enlightened man and ruler of a half district of Jerusalem. He was a learned man who knew the importance of the father in the home. He did not just leave his daughters to do "women's work" at home or to be the sole responsibility of their mother but he took them with him to see what he did. If he was building, he showed them how to build and they helped him as much as any male child would. If he was in the office, I am sure they were allowed to see that side too. Shallum understood that a woman who is able to take her place comfortably in the world in any place that is right for her is helped by a father who says "yes you can, that's my girl". Do not allow your husband to abdicate responsibility for the children. It is very important in the life of children that their father is able to give them confidence in who they are, give them approval in what they can do and give them permission to be who they choose to be. What a great start for any child, male or female. In the case of males, they need father as a role model. In the case of females, they need father to give them confidence to go out there and they need father to give them a good picture of the kind of man that is best for their lives, one who will allow them to be themselves, not one who will abuse them and tell them they are worthless and do not amount to much.

And if you do not have such a father? Well you do. If you do not have such an earthly father, you have your heavenly one. But I have to say it is easier to have both.

# PROFESSIONAL AND BUSINESS WOMEN

*A (hu)man's aim shall be higher than his grasp*
*Or what's the heavens for?*
*Robert Browning – Andrea del Sarto*

*I Chronicles 7:20-24*

Builders, Government officials, warriors, Judges and heroines? Whatever next? Were women learned all those years ago? Could they take on intellectual activity that early on? Well of course.

Once upon a time, there lived Sherah the daughter of Ephraim. No, she was not a cartoon character. She really did live. She was the daughter of Ephraim. Ephraim and Manasseh were the two sons of Joseph of the amazing technicolour dreamcoat. Because of their father Joseph, their tribe had a pretty special place amongst their people. But Sherah never got much of a look in because her father Ephraim seemed only interested in his sons. Her story is sandwiched between the numerous genealogies of the twelve tribes because it was that important. Many have missed this significant story but for the purposes of this study the Holy Spirit led me to Sherah.

Ephraim had many sons and two of them had very sadly been killed by the Philistines when they went down to seize their livestock. They were clearly macho men, going on expeditions which included seizing other people's livestock, probably as a result of some feud or other that they refused to resolve. Their father understandably mourned for many days. There is no mention of their mother mourning although she must have been heartbroken.

After the period of mourning, Ephraim's immediate instinct was to replace the sons he had lost and his wife became pregnant again. He must have been comforted when the new baby turned out to be another boy.

There is no mention of his little girl Sherah until the very last verse in the story of this family. The Bible makes a statement which I found shocking at the time. It says,

"His daughter was Sherah who built Lower and Upper Beth Horon as well as Uzzen Sherah."

Wow! All those years ago, there was this woman called Sherah who built three cities and one of them was named after her! How come no one ever tells us the Bible contains such history?

Sherah's family descendants from Joseph were clearly of the educated and the elite in the days when Egypt was so advanced in mathematics and civilisation that she was building the pyramids. The family and descendants of Joseph had better opportunities than others to learn science and mathematics and other intellectual pursuits of the times. They clearly did. The one thing we know about the Hebrews is that they excelled wherever they went and whatever they did because they approached everything with diligence and commitment and a strong base in God. They learnt whatever there was to learn and applied it as well or even better than other people.

I have to take my hat off to Ephraim because he

obviously tried to teach his macho sons mathematics. I have to take my hat off to him because even though there was not much mention of the female Sherah until the last verse, he must have included her in these studies and allowed her to excel. She did not disappoint. She scaled the heights of learning to become an architect. The daughters of Shullah helped their father to build the wall and were probably helpful in his town planning office for half the district but Sherah was the Architect and master planner who built three cities.

# THE VIRTUOUS WOMAN

*Where'er you walk*
*Cool gales shall fan the glade*
*Trees where you sit*
*Shall crowd into a shade*
*Trees where you sit shall fan into a shade*
*Where'er you tread, the blushing flowers shall rise*
*And all things flourish, where'er you turn your eyes*
*Where'er you turn your eyes*
      *Handel's aria from* Semele

*Proverbs Chapter 31:10-31*

When I was a little girl aged only about 13, I was very ill and as a result of a very high fever became delirious. I began to spout passages from Proverbs 31 which my mother had taught me. So impressed was I with these verses of scripture that my fevered brain could think of nothing more important to spout. In those days in Christian families, schools and Sunday school, children were encouraged to memorise scripture, psalms such as psalm 23, the Apostles Creed, the Catechism, various prayers of the Common Prayer book and scriptural and religious verses of significance. In those days Christianity played a role in the upbringing of children, much more so than today. Today we speak about broken societies. I wonder why. Perhaps we should follow the biblical instructions. Teach the child the way that he should go and when he grows up he will not forget it.

There is no better way of dealing with the qualities of this woman other than to read the text itself. I simply want to comment that amongst her many virtues, she seems to me to be a well established and successful business woman. She selects wool and flax and works with eager hands. Perhaps she has a textile business which produces only the very best materials. She orders her food from afar, perhaps she is an international trader. She seems to be in real estate too. She considers a field and buys it, we are told. She certainly works very hard, is well organised and she sees that her trading is profitable. Like Esther she is very well dressed and seems to make the most of her looks without being frivolous or flighty. She clearly does not spend all her time on beautifying herself, since she is so busy but spends just enough time to look her best. Her home is equally well turned out.

She not only makes textiles on a large scale, she has a designing business also and even supplies to other merchants.

This is a woman who makes it clear to us that with wisdom, good organisation and the setting of priorities, we can have it all. She does not ignore her household in all these business enterprises. No. Her husband is very happy with her. Her children think she is the best mother ever. Her home is a priority, very comfortable and well run. She has it all.

Her secret? This is in verse 30

"Charm is deceptive, and beauty is fleeting, but a woman who fears the Lord is to be praised."

The God of Abraham Jacob and Isaac was her centre. She feared the Lord and walked in his ways and relied on him for wisdom. She obeyed his commands and lived by his standards. She had true wisdom which comes from learning the wisdom of God. She was not idle and she cared for others because the love of Jehovah was in her heart. She gave to the poor and did not just give and care for those who were part of her own household or her own circle.

One very important lesson to be learned about this highly successful business woman is that her husband was not a house-husband. Her husband was not an under-achiever. Many women have made the mistake in this modern age of thinking that we can role swap. It simply does not work. Whether we like it or not, there are differences between men and women. We have many similarities as homo sapiens but we also have many differences. Women as child bearers tend to be more gifted in nurturing and nesting and men who are not made to carry children, have different qualities. It is a sad aspect of modern day feminism that these things are not taken on board. We are all the same they shout. Well we jolly well are not. What is important to note is that our differences do not make us inferior. We can all do anything depending on what God has given each of us to do but there are differences between men and women in emotions, physique, and in many other subtle ways. There are of course many similarities. I do not think women need to try and be like men to prove themselves. Just prove yourself as a woman. Have your own style as a woman. You do not have to emulate a man. Prove yourself as a woman. Be proud of your womanhood.

If you turn him into a house-husband in total, he will turn round and hate you because nature did not create him to be house bound. Nature did not create anybody to be house bound but we must accept that women as the child bearers are more gifted with the nesting instinct. I do not suggest that women only should do the housework, no way. A man must help but it is a reality that there are certain things that women naturally do better than men and can lead or spearhead that, for instance, organising the home. But the important lesson here is not to turn your husband into or allow him to be an underachiever. Even if he is lazy, believe in him, encourage him and help him. Be a team. Be true partners in life. Do not compete with him like Vashti did with her husband and do not let him compete with you. In love understand that the achievement of one is a feather in the cap of the other.

The virtuous woman was a great success in everything. But so was her husband. It says that he not only sat amongst the elders of the land which must be similar to being a member of the House of Lords or some equivalent, but was respected amongst them. That is one of the reasons why this relationship worked. He had realised his potential too and had not been put in the shade by a highly successful and enterprising wife.

Like Deborah the Judge, prophet and warrior, who for all her giddy heights of achievement was known as the wife of Lappidoth, the virtuous woman was the wife of Lord Virtue.

# BAD GIRLS

*Angels are bright still though the brightest fell*
*Though all things foul will wear the brows of grace*
*Yet grace must still look so.*
　　　　*William Shakespeare* – Macbeth

There are some bad girls mentioned in the Bible that are relevant studies for decent women but only a few. For some reasons bad girls seem to take centre stage. Mention women in the Bible and most people immediately think of Jezebel, Delilah, Herodias, murder, intrigue, seduction and evil. I have only one thing to say about the three women mentioned here. They worshipped other gods. They did not know Jehovah, the only God of goodness, love and holiness. How could they be anything else? If the root of the tree is bad, its fruit will be bad but if the root of the tree is good, the fruit will be good. No, I have nothing to say about these kind of women. They cannot be anything else but bad. But there were other bad girls, really bad girls who did not remain bad. Of them I will speak as they teach all of us that it is possible to change. It is not how you started that counts, it is how you finished. She who perseveres till the end will be saved.

# BATHSHEBA

The sacrifices of God are a broken spirit, a broken
and a contrite heart , O God thou wilt not despise
Psalm 51:16

*II Samuel Chapters 11 and 12*

Was she an adulteress who seduced a king? Who goes
to the top of their house to bathe knowing that the
King's palace is within view and they could be seen
from the palace windows? Someone who wanted to be
seen perhaps, who knows? These are questions some
people ask about Bathsheba. Whether she initiated
being seduced by King David or whether she was
innocently bathing on the roof as part of rites of
purification, she slept with him willingly enough even
though her very own husband was one of his
prominent commanders. She raised no objections.

In laying some responsibility on Bathsheba, I must
make it clear that I believe that the greater sin was
David's. David was much older than Bathsheba and
he was the King. What on earth was he doing sleeping
with the wife of one of his generals and mighty men?
However except in cases of rape both parties have
sinned, whoever initiated it. This story has many
lessons in it for us women. One of those lessons is that
we have a responsibility for what we do, how we
dress, how much of ourselves we expose and how we
conduct ourselves in male company. Whilst there is no
indication in the biblical text that Bathsheba knew she

was being watched as she bathed, it is a good lesson for us to be sensible and thoughtful in how we conduct ourselves.

When she got pregnant the king sent for her husband and allowed him leave from the army. The idea was that the child to be borne would be passed off as his. But Uriah the Hittite was a man who preferred to fight men's wars rather than spend time lazing about with his wife when there was a war on. It is likely that Bathsheba was neglected and starved of love in her personal life but that does not give her the right to seek it elsewhere. She was an adulteress and sinner in her relationship with David. She was however no murderer because there is no evidence whatsoever that she knew or even suspected what David was about to do next.

When Uriah the Hittite returned to the war front refusing to skive off when the army needed him, David gave instructions that he was to be put into the thick of battle and then abandoned. The inevitable result was his death. And so died Uriah the Hittite with no one to mourn him but an unfaithful wife whose heart already belonged to another.

What is clear and amazing is that although God punished them both with the death of the child, God clearly forgave them both and not only forgave them but blessed them with a son who became the wisest and wealthiest King in the world. That Solomon was the son of Bathsheba and David never fails to amaze me. With God, once you have truly repented, his forgiveness is as if the sin never happened. Bathsheba had four sons and of all of them went on to greatness. She was loved by God as she had been forgiven by God.

"As far as the east is from the west so far shall I remove your transgressions from you."

Bathsheba turned from an unfaithful wife into a faithful and wise woman who loved her King and husband and coped well with Palace life. Her repentance and that of David were clearly true and God completely forgave them. It is not how you started that counts, it is how you finish. Her son Solomon was known all over the world for his wisdom and in his youth for his devotion to Jehovah God. This he must have learned not only from his father King David but from his mother also. Bathsheba learned her lesson and never put a foot wrong again. She lived the rest of her life as an exemplary wife to King David and a great mother to Prince Solomon. There is indication in the scriptures that David relied much on her for advice. There are indications that even the sons of other wives of David honoured Bathsheba and she was kind and gracious to them.

The great lesson for us all in this story is that adultery is a deadly evil and will result in heartache, despair and even death. Every sin that a man commits is outside his or her body but the adulterous man or woman sins against their own body. St Paul urges us to fight the devil in all kinds of ways except in the area of adultery and fornication. In this area, he urges us to run. "Flee fornication", he said, understanding full well that you dip your toe in the water and there comes a time when you may be unable to say "No", even if you want to. The best thing to do is to run and not get to that point at all. From the moment Bathsheba decided to bathe on her roof, their fate was sealed and it had to take a drastic step of running in the opposite direction for her and King David to avoid what happened. The suffering that King David and Bathsheba went through was not just limited to the death of Uriah and their child, the intense pain and regret that must have brought, the shame of the open rebuke of the prophet Nathan, but went further. It is as if the act of adultery opened the door to the devil into David's family and the suffering knew no end. The story carries on to tell of the incest of one of his sons and the rape of his daughter. His son Absalom dealt with that by killing Amnon his brother and later revolting against his Dad who did not properly deal with the incest and rape. Sin opens the door for the enemy into our homes. Is any sin worth the price we pay for it? Every disobedience of God carries consequences, even if only to give the enemy the right to attack you and yours.

The second great lesson from this story is that adultery is not necessarily the end of the road. It is the one sin that the Lord accepts can lead to divorce, but even when he said this, he made it clear that forgiveness is possible between the affected couple, so long as they are honest and sincere with each other and truly repent of their sin. Adultery is a terrible thing to get over in a marriage. When you find out, a picture gets into your heard which may take years to get rid of, even when you are willing to make another go of it with your spouse. God is not a kill joy and does not call certain things sin for no good reason. His good reason is that he wants to spare us all the hurt and pain that it brings. In this story David and Bathsheba lost their son. Bathsheba lost her husband and must have guessed what happened, how he died. But in their case, their repentance was true. The Lord saw to it, when he sent the prophet Nathan to tell David that God knew what he had done. David mourned and fasted and put on sackcloth and it was for real. The matter was not hidden but came to light for everyone to know. What pain they must have gone through. But they kept faith with the Lord and won through. God is a forgiving God after all to those who truly repent. And when he forgives, following true repentance, it is as if it never happened. Bathsheba made restitution for what she did, as did King David, by becoming a far different type of woman from the one she was when it all happened.

# RAHAB

*Come now let us reason together says the Lord*
*Though your sins be as scarlet*
*They shall be white as snow*
*Though they be red like crimson*
*They shall be as wool*

Isaiah 1:18

Joshua 2

Rahab was a prostitute. The two spies sent by Joshua to spy out Canaan ended up in her apartment where many men before them ended up, it would seem. But what happened with the spies was very different from her usual activities.

This woman, however, seems to be a prostitute with a difference. She read the papers and did not just saunter through life taking money and drugs and unaware of things happening around her. This particular prostitute was compos mentis and when the two spies came to her house, she knew who they were. She knew that this tribe of Isreal had been undefeated by all the armies of the nations round about her. She must have researched their religion and found that their God was different from the gods of the nations around. She had the good sense to realise that the God of Israel must be the supreme being.

This girl was smart. She knew which side her bread was buttered on. After she had misdirected the security police that came after the two spies, she went up to where she had hidden them in the roof of her house and said,

"I know your God is greater than all the other gods because you have won all the battles you have fought. We have even heard how you took the great city of Jericho without firing a single shot. I want to be on your side. I want to know this God."

The biblical account of this story makes it clear that Rahab had heard, through interest of an alert and enquiring mind, of the wonderful exploits and victory that the children of Israel had been given wherever they went over forty years in the wilderness. She referred to every single one. She took the trouble to find out and to know about that which is good.

I like to think that Rahab was a reluctant prostitute, one who fell into this dreadful trade because at the time it looked as if she had no choice. At the time she did not know God and did not know how to seek other alternatives. It would appear that she not only traded or worked in flax, indicating that indeed she did whatever work she could get and did not just take prostitution as the easy way out, but it would also appear that she cared for her family. Indeed when the way out presented itself, she asked for salvation for her family also not just for herself. By this I am sure she meant her extended family as well as any children she had. Rahab may even have been a widow in a country where there were no provisions for the women and sheer desperation led her into her sordid trade. But it really does not matter whether she was a half -hearted prostitute or whether she was the mother of all prostitutes. When she saw a chance to repent and turn to worship the true God in holiness and in truth she took it and God took her back.

"Tie a red ribbon round your house," the spies said, "so that when we come to destroy the rest, you and your house and all within the safe enclosure of the red ribbon will be spared from destruction."

Rahab did as they said and she and her household were spared by the children of God.

"Put the blood of the lamb upon your doors and your lintels and when the Angel of death passes by, you will be spared", Moses had said to the children of Israel on the eve of the tenth plague and the destruction of the first born sons of the household of those outside the blood.

The children of Israel did as Moses said and were spared their first born sons.

This echoes forward to the New Testament and the work of the paschal lamb, Jesus himself, who came to earth to die and shed his blood for the salvation and deliverance of whosoever wishes to accept it.

Ephesians 1:7 says "In him we have redemption through his blood, the forgiveness of our sins in accordance with the wisdom of God's grace that he lavished upon us."

This blood for the forgiveness of sins is for whosoever wishes to accept it. Jesus is the lamb of God that was slain for the forgiveness of the sins of man, reconciliation to God and deliverance from all darkness.

Rahab's red ribbon, like the blood on the lintels was an echo of the sacrifice to come. It was only an echo and not the real thing but it was enough at the time as it was done in obedience to God and therefore an acceptable sacrifice to him. Those who obey save their lives and the lives of their loved ones.

Rahab, like everyone of us can, by turning to God and his provision for salvation, was able to save herself and be an instrument of salvation for her family. She developed an interest in knowing the true God, sought him and found him and never let him go.

God did not forget this former prostitute. In the genealogy of Christ according to the book of Matthew the Bible does something of note. Two women are unusually mentioned. One of them is the Moabitess Ruth and the other is the former prostitute Rahab. Just incase anyone wants to remind Rahab about her previous sordid life, as far as the Lord is concerned, it is as if it never happened. If anyone is in Christ she is a new creation, the old has passed, the new has come. It is not how we started but how we finish that counts and she who endures till the end, will be saved. The Lord was proud to show in his human genealogy this former prostitute as his ancestor.

# LEAH

*And I will make of thee a great nation*
*And I will bless thee and make thy name great*
*And thou shall be a blessing......*
*And in thee shall all the families of the earth be blessed*
Genesis 12 :1-3

Genesis 28 – 35

Leah was ugly or so she was told. To make matters worse, her younger sister was beautiful. Rachel was every girl's dream of how they would like to look. She had beautiful features, beautiful manners, dainty feet, a neat waist and a gentle languid voice. She was a happy girl always laughing effortlessly. Everyone loved Rachel.

"How are we ever going to get you married Leah?" her father Laban, openly complained.

Leah buried her lack of confidence in hard work and diligence and tried to get along as best as she could with her ever popular sister.

But as if that wasn't enough, they both fell in love with the same man.

Jacob was on the run from his brother Essau whose birthright Essau believed Jacob had stolen. Jacob was taken in by the family and he lived happily with them working for them as a shepherd. But it did not take long for him to fall hopelessly in love with Rachel. He asked for her hand in marriage and was given it by Laban. But the crafty old so and so swapped the girls on the wedding night substituting Leah instead.

How Leah could have taken her sister's place knowing how much she and Jacob loved each other never fails to amaze me. But she did. She was callous and selfish and took her sister's man. That was not nice.

She did not get Jacob's heart. Whilst he was married to her and he was having children by her, he carried on wooing Rachel. Unfortunately Rachel died in childbirth when she had Benjamin and Leah at last had a chance to have something. I doubt that she ever had it though. Jacob's love for Rachel transferred into a special love for her two children Joseph and Benjamin. I would like to say that in this story something amazing happened that changed everything but I rather suspect that Leah continued to suffer in one way or the other for what she had done to her sister. It is quite clear that she did not manage to create any great love for the children of Rachel amongst her own flesh born sons either as her own attitudes transferred to them. They were unloving enough to wish to kill Joseph. The bitterness of their mother spilled over to them. But there is one great thing that can be said about Ruth and that is that her fourth son was called Judah which means God be praised. I like to think that it was not just how Jacob felt at the time after getting so many sons but truly how Leah felt. She may be denied the full love of her husband but she had the full love of God and recognised it at that stage. And the God of mercy to whom each one of us is beautiful honoured dear Leah by making her the mother of a nation. Of the twelve tribes of the nation from whom came The Christ, ten of them were borne by ugly Leah who may not have looked so nice to man but to her loving God she was practically perfect, in looks anyway and became even better when she turned her heart to praise God following the birth of Judah.

As the virtuous woman said

"Charm is deceitful and beauty is vain but a woman who fears the Lord, that woman is to be praised. Give her the reward she has earned, and let her works bring her praise at the city gate." Proverbs 31:30-31

# SPIRITUAL WOMEN

I have proved once and for all in the story of Deborah
that a woman can be the spiritual and/or temporal
head of a nation under the Judaeo/Christian God. But
just in case some say that one exception does not make
the rule, I will look at other examples here.

# HULDAH THE PROPHETESS

*Thy word is a lamp unto my feet*
*And a light unto my path*
Psalm 119:105

## 2 Kings Chapter 22

Josiah was a boy king. He took the throne at the age of eight. There had been times of terrible upheaval prior to his ascendancy of the throne. The temple was in disrepair but the boy King decided to repair it. One day someone foraging amongst the dust and ruins found a book.

"Whatever is this?" the King asked.

In all the land no one could be found who could tell the young and curious King what the book was except the prophetess Huldah. She had kept faith in the midst of ever growing darkness. She had held on to her belief in and knowledge of Jehovah. She alone had held the fort when everyone else had given in. How she must have prayed and prayed and prayed again. The Lord heard her and at the appointed time, she was called upon to explain to the young King and his Ministers the Law and the Prophets and to teach once again the word of the living God. It was to her that the palace and everyone else referred for spiritual knowledge. She was effectively the spiritual leader of the nation at the time and God allowed it to be so. She was the centre of the Revival in the reign of Josiah the boy King, and a spiritual leader just as Deborah had been all those years ago.

# THE SHUNEMITE

*When peace like a river attendeth my way*
*When sorrow like strong billows blow*
*Whatever my state, thou hast taught me to say*
*It is well, it is well with my soul*
                                        Hymns Ancient and Modern

This lady is one of my favourite characters in the Bible. She was a woman of great faith. She was a woman with great spiritual insight, a woman who loved her husband and with him created a fine and well run home that was welcoming and inviting to others including the prophet Elisha.

It is true that the greatest battles are won when the Deborahs join with the Baraks and the Jaels and other foot soldiers play their part, of course it is. But I have found spiritually that women have a spiritual insight often sharper than the men. A woman is often the first person to spot a potential danger to her home. There is no secret to this. It is as the Lord established it. As far back as the garden of Eden and the fall of man the Lord said

"I have put special enmity between the woman and the snake."

Yes, we women can discern especially when it concerns our homes. That is one of the reasons why the Lord counselled Abraham to listen to his wife when Sarah made an important suggestion regarding the future of Ishmael and Hagar. She knew probably with great regret that it would never work out with too many cooks making the broth. Herself and Haggar were one too many female cooks in the household kitchen. One had to go.

When the Shunemite saw Elisha, it was she not her husband that recognised the man of God for who he was. She persuaded her husband not only to accept this man but to build a little annexe for the prophet. She was clearly a woman loved and trusted by her husband to be able to persuade him to do this. She read her newspapers and knew what was happening in her country at the time and the power of the woman Jezebel and the prophets of Baal. She knew that she had to protect Elisha. She also knew that the prophet needed time to pray and could not just be a guest living any old how with them and fitting into their ordinary household. She knew that the prophet had to come and go and did not hold on to him. She recognised that he had assignments that she and her family could not be part of. They never stood in the prophet's way as they gave him shelter and protection at great danger to themselves, it must be said. Jezebel would have had a lot to say about guarding any prophet especially Elisha. All Israel must have known Ahab and Jezebel were looking for this man. But the Shunemite and her husband took the risk and supplied the prophet with whatever he needed by way of funds, food, equipment and time.

They asked for nothing in return, but our good God is no one's debtor. He rewards all those who diligently seek him. No one can out-give God from whom all blessings flow. There is nothing wrong with giving to God's work with expectation of reward for yourself but there is a far better place and that is to give and not to count the cost, to give and not to ask for any reward save that of knowing that we do the will of God. Giving for the sheer joy of pleasing our Father is a wonderful place for a Christian to be.

They never asked the prophet for anything but it did not take a genius for the prophet to see that the perfect household was lacking a child. He prayed for the Shunemite and she became pregnant after all the years of hoping and praying. How joyful she must have been. She must have been quite something as a woman to live happily with her husband and be in a position to persuade him to build a new annexe to house a nationally controversial man, even though she had born her husband no children. This was not a marriage made for the purposes of having children but this was a marriage of love between the two parties which was so strong that it transcended the misfortune of not being able to have children.

So a child was born. The prophet came and went and their idyllic life continued, even happier than before.

One day the father took the child to the fields with him. This man must have been a very wealthy man to be able to provide for the prophet in the way he did. Their fields must have been worked professionally. There were other workers who worked for him so we are looking at some large scale farming operation here.

The picture of the father taking his son to his place of work is a very good one. We have seen a similar picture with the daughters of Shullah who helped their father to build the wall of Jerusalem under the prophet Nehemiah. A father is very important in the life of any child, male or female but in the life of a male child, he is doubly important because he is a direct role model. Nature has made women producers of children and that is a fact that can never be changed. Women therefore are generally more in the role of nurturers in the home. Fathers are more important in the areas of introducing the child to the world outside the home. These are not clear-cut demarcations but they are in the main the family models that work well. Even where mother is a professional, it is important that father has a role in this area of introducing the child to the outside world and how it works. This is what was happening in this family. I think the rest of the book should make it clear that I am not arguing that women should be housewives only but I am arguing that women should be nurturers whether they are full time housewives or not.

When the child became sick, it was the natural thing for the father to ask for him to be taken to his mother whose nurturing role took precedence in the circumstances. He had every confidence in his wife. She would know what to do. I am sure he did not realise how seriously ill the child was or he would have come home himself. As far as he could see, the child needed his mother who would know what to do. The illness was probably meningitis or something similar as it caught hold and progressed very quickly indeed.

The Shunemite did not disappoint her husband. Even when the child died, she knew what to do. I love this woman who even in the face of a dead child did not crumble into jelly but full of determination and urgency saddled her horse. She did not wait for her husband to return as many of us would, playing martyr and helpless victim. She was never helpless. Her husband could always rely on her to get things done and she came up trumps every time.

She rode to find the prophet and when she saw him, he said, sensing in his spirit that something was wrong,

"Is it well with you, Shunemite? Is it well with your family?"

And she answered with one of the most profound, amazing and faith inspiring words in the Bible.

"It is well."

She had a dead child upstairs in her bedroom at home but she said "It is well." Top that for faith. This woman knew that she would never allow the devil to take from her anything that God had given her.

Was there anxiety in Elisha's question enquiring after the family that he had come to love so much? Probably. He was a prophet after all. When the Shunemite had confirmed his suspicion he returned immediately with her to pray over the body of the child. Hades gave up that which did not belong to it and the child lived again!

What a woman! A woman who refused to let the devil take from her what God had given her. A woman who had the discernment not only to recognise the man of God but the action of God. Why would God take her son away? No she said to Hades. No, my son shall live again. And he did.

I note that when the prophet offered his servant Gehazi to go with her to pray about the problem, she refused his offer. She would not be fobbed off with an also ran. I also like to think that her discernment ability did not desert her because she sensed something about Gehazi who was later proved to be a thief and sacked from his position as the prophet's assistant. Gehazi later went behind his master's back to accept in circumstances which amounted to stealing the gifts of Naaman of the Syrian army.

This is not the end of the story of the Shunemite because she became a legend in her own times. There came a time when her son had grown up and she had to go into exile with him. She was warned by the prophet to go because of the famine that was coming upon the land. She was an obedient woman and went in accordance with the word of the prophet. When they returned from exile her properties had been taken from her and the farmlands of her husband were taken by squatters. She wanted them back and as usual her courage and faith in God did not desert her. She went up to the King to ask for her land back.

God was watching over her and her son as he always did and the heavenly Father himself arranged one of the finest examples of a divine appointment in the Bible. Just at the time she went up to speak to the King, the King was at that very time discussing with his officials tales of this Shunemite whose son the prophet had raised from the dead. Just as they were speaking, in walks the very woman to confirm the story herself, with her very alive son walking next to her. The King was captivated by the whole story and gave her back her land and everything else that she owned with interest. Wow! This is a woman that never allowed the enemy to take away from her anything that God had given her.

"I will give back the years the locust has eaten," says the Lord.

May we, like the Shunemite, learn how to hold on to the promises of God in faith and take back all that the devil has stolen from us.

One of the greatest hymns of all time was based on the story of the Shunemite and it is one that is worth remembering, for faith is the evidence of things not seen, the assurance of things hoped for and without faith it is impossible to please God. We must learn not to look at the circumstances but at the power of the Almighty, most gracious, most merciful, omnipresent, omniscient God. Faith is simply trusting and believing that his word is true and he will never lie. He can do all things. Did he not create everything? Nothing is impossible with God.

The hymn continues

Chorus
It is well, it is well.
With my soul, with my soul
It is well, it is well with my soul.

My sin, oh the bliss of this glorious thought!
My sin, not in part but in whole
Is nailed to His cross and I bear it no more
Praise the Lord, praise the Lord O my soul.

For me be it Christ, be it Christ hence to live!
If Jordan above me shall roll
No pang shall be mine. For in death as in life,
Thou wilt whisper thy peace to my soul.

But Lord 'tis for thee, for thy coming, we wait
The sky not the grave is our goal
O trump of the Angel! O voice of the Lord!
Blessed hope! Blessed rest of my soul!

# HANNAH THE PRAYER WARRIOR

*He prayeth best who loveth best*
*All things both great and small*
*For the dear Lord who loveth all*
*He made and loveth all*

Samuel Taylor Coleridge
*Rhyme of the Ancient Mariner*

## 1 Samuel Chapter 1

She was another lady who did not have children. Her husband had two wives and it did not help that Peninnah with her many children did not make life easy for poor lonely Hannah. Peninnah's "in your face" behaviour constantly reminded the lady Hannah of her great desire and need to have a child of her own.

Hannah knew God and knew that God could do anything. She prayed so fervently whilst everyone else was out partying, for the gift of a child. She prayed with such abandon that the priest thought she was drunk. The Lord answered and she gave birth to Samuel, one of the greatest prophets of Israel, dedicated from birth by a devout mother to the God that had given her special favour to be the mother of the prophet.

The Lord Jesus said,

"Ask and it shall be given unto you, seek and you shall find."

Prayer is an essential weapon for all Christians and all those who are serious with God and who know him. Whatever the trouble, take it to the Lord in prayer. And the God that answereth by fire will answer you from his Holy Mountain Zion.

Samuel was totally precious to a woman whose husband had married another woman to give him children and this other woman Peninnah had produced so many children! What did Hannah do with the only child she had? She gave him back to the Lord. She did not just do this metaphorically, she actually sent him away to live in the Temple quarters with Eli the priest. What a sacrifice, a life sacrifice and in return the Lord blessed Hannah most abundantly and made her son one of the greatest prophets and Judges of Israel. Upheld by his mother's prayers, how could he go wrong? He never did. Samuel was respected and honoured throughout all Israel and began to hear God from a very young age. Even when Israel had their first King, King Saul, it was still to Samuel that all Isreal and the King looked for advice, guidance and counsel. Hannah got her heart's desire but not to show off with. With her, as with all the women in these studies, it was "God first". With God first you get the best. Jesus said "Seek ye first the kingdom of God and his righteousness and all these things shall be added unto you."

# HOUSEWIVES AND CARERS

*Wither thou goest, I will go*
*Where thou lodgest, I will lodge*
*Thy people shall be my people, and thy God my God.*
*Where thou diest will I die*
*And there will I be buried*

Ruth 1:15-17

The Book of Ruth

I have made the point very clearly in this book that because of our biological child bearing abilities, we have a greater tendency than men towards nesting. We are born with it. We are made physically more adaptable to some of these home tasks. Men on the other hand, made from the dust of the earth are much more outdoors orientated, workwise and playwise (we are one step removed from the dust and made from the rib of the man).

Despite having been at University with my husband where we both graduated in law and despite 30 years as a qualified and very busy Barrister, in the home it is I who am more aware of how the home is run. With love and patience (most of the time) I have shown my husband how to do various things in the house to the extent that he can almost cope with anything without me. I still have to organise and sometimes initiate but he is now a very willing sharer of household chores at any level and quite capable of doing it all. For a man whose mother did not teach him how to wash a dish, this is quite an achievement. I thank God that I did not give up the ghost when he was unable to do certain things in the home and I thank God that I did not think he was pretending or taking advantage or thinking that only women did housework or any of the other bitter thoughts that I could have succumbed to. He just did not know how or understand it all. I thank God that he was willing to learn and to help and when necessary now, for instance if I am not well, he can even take over.

There was the case of one woman who wanted to divorce her husband because she would send him out to the shops telling him what to buy and he would come back with only half of it and not remember the rest. The silly goose was very distressed by this and concluded her husband did not love her because he did not pay attention to her shopping list. When presented with her problem some of my friends said the solution was to write him a list. I was less charitable "Do the blinking shopping yourself, you dozy cow" was my response. Well, in my head, anyway.

The point I seek to make here is that women are naturally more gifted at caring and organising the home than men. There will of course be exceptions. Gordon Ramsay's wife probably does very little cooking but I am quite sure that everything else is majorly organised by her. There is nothing wrong with a woman being a housewife and a carer because organising the home is as important as anything else that we have to do to make life worth living. In fact it is one of the most important areas.

Ruth was a carer and a housewife. She had

married her Jewish husband when he came to live in her country in Moab. Unfortunately, he had died and his mother Naomi wished to return to her people and her home in Judea. She called her two daughters in law Ruth and Oprah and gave them the freedom to stay in their country rather than return to Judea with her. Her reasoning was sound and selfless. Far from putting herself and her need first and seeking, in the girls, someone to look after her in her old age, she put the two girls first. They were young and needed to re-marry. She did not have any male relations who would be suitable husbands for them. Besides they would probably be happier in their own country amongst their own people and in their own culture.

Ruth had clearly become a proselyte before her marriage, otherwise the marriage would never have taken place. She had come, through her husband, to the knowledge of the one true God and had taken this new God for herself whilst her people all around her worshipped idols. Ruth, when given the option to stay with her idol worshipping people, refused. She would rather go into permanent widowhood and poverty with Naomi, she would rather spend her time caring for the heart-broken and aging mother-in-law who was for good reason no longer a bundle of laughs with her two boys dead and no grandchildren. Anything was better than running the risk of losing her new faith.

"I will never leave you nor turn from following after you," she vowed to Naomi.

Her words are now famous words as many who have ever been married will confirm. Those words of total commitment form part of many marriage ceremonies. But it is not for this alone that Ruth is known.

Back in Judea, those who saw Naomi after her return were shocked at how much she had altered, how much suffering had changed her. They barely recognised the handsome adventurous mother of two fine sons in the person of the emaciated sad wreck of a woman.

"Is this Naomi?" they pondered with incredulity.

Well it was. Losing your two sons in a foreign country does take it out of you. But she had Ruth and gradually the old Naomi began to return and resurface. Her loving thoughts turned to the future of the daughter-in-law who had given up such a lot in giving up her own people and family to follow her into poverty and oblivion because she loved her and she loved her God.

"What are we going to do to get her married?" she said to herself.

Ruth had dutifully been going gleaning. They had no money and they could only rely on the provision for the poor as commanded by the Lord in Leviticus 19:9-10.

"Do not take all the corn when you harvest. Spare some for the gleaners," said the Lord.

It is interesting to note that the gleaners still had to work in the fields to get this corn left for them. It was not all done and wrapped and tinned and delivered to their door as modern day governments do in their social security provisions. The Bible recognises how important it is for people do things for themselves and the command was for provision for the poor in circumstances where the poor had to work hard too to get that which was provided for them. That way no one ever takes anything for granted or makes the mistake of thinking that they can sit on their backsides doing nothing and everyone else owes them a living.

Young Ruth worked hard as a gleaner. She did not mind that it was work for the poor. She did not feel bitter about those who took the cream of the crop whilst they had the left overs. The crop was theirs after all and they had worked hard to build what they had. She was only grateful that some of the people who had more than enough were godly enough to obey the commandments of God so that people like her could be catered for. Ruth must also have taken care of herself, keeping herself clean, keeping her looks as well as she could under the circumstances of poverty. Style does not always mean money. That must be so because Boaz noticed her and showed her kindness. He noticed her beauty, her demeanor, her hardwork and he eventually noticed the fact that she had given up her potential for a better life amongst her own people so she could come home with Naomi and look after her and worship her new God Jehovah with the people of Jehovah.

One day Naomi called Ruth to one side and said,

"That man who showed you kindness is our kinsman." She sensed, as only women can, the potential here. Although they were poor Boaz was a relation who could marry Ruth and he was not bad looking. With the care of Ruth the loving scheming of Naomi reared its head.

"When the work is done today, wait till Boaz has eaten and when he is asleep, go and lie by his foot."

Well this was far beyond a hint. Ruth trusted Naomi and did as she was told. There is no hint in the scriptures that anything happened between them that night before the right time. There are indeed times when we have to take bold and controversial steps to achieve the right end. But we must be careful to do everything in holiness and with the right motive. The rest is history. Boaz married her and not only did he marry her but their son was Obed the son of Jesse, the father of David the greatest King of Israel.

But it was not just the Royal line of Israel and Judah that came from the womb of Ruth, a foreign woman, a Moabitess. At the appointed time the King of Kings came from the Royal House of Jehovah and dwelt in the womb of a descendant of the house of David. Her name was Mary and she bore a son named Jesus the King of Kings and Lord of Lords.

In the genealogy of Jesus in the book of Matthew Chapter 1, two women are mentioned. One is Rahab to whom I have already referred and the other is Ruth the Moabitess, the ancestor of the Saviour.

# BATTERED WIVES

*But now thus saith the Lord, that created thee.......*
*Fear not, for I have redeemed thee. I have called thee by thy*
*name thou art mine*
*When thou walkest through the waters, I will be with thee:*
*And through the rivers they shall not overwhelm thee:*
*When thou passeth through the fire thou shalt not be*
*burned*
*Neither shall the flame kindle against thee.*
*Since you are precious in my sight and you have been*
*honourable and I have loved thee*
*Therefore will I give men for thee and people in exchange*
*for your life.*

Isaiah 42:1-4


## I Samuel 25

His name was Nabal and he was a fool by name and a
fool by nature. He was cruel to his wife Abigail.
Abigail, the Bible tells us, was beautiful and kind and
good. Her husband's treatment of her did not arise
from anything she had done. He was just a brute. I am
quite sure he beat her as well, although we are not told
that. Whether it was physical or emotional cruelty, or
both, the Bible is clear on the point. Nabal was a fool,
a bad husband, a bad man. He wasn't just bad to his
wife, he was bad to everyone, one of those bad
tempered ill humoured men that no one except serving
wenches in cheap bars can please. Despite the fact that
David had looked after his livestock as a gesture of

goodwill whilst he was a fugitive in the area, Nabal would not return the goodwill by giving David and his men any help when they needed it. No was not sufficient for the ungracious Nabal. He had to throw in a few gratuitous words of abuse with his refusal. All of Israel knew that David had killed Goliath in battle and thereby disabled the army of Philistia by taking out their greatest and most feared general. Everyone knew that Saul, the King had gone mad with jealousy and was chasing David to kill him, although David had done nothing but good to the nation and to King Saul and his family. But none of that mattered to Nabal. It was not about right and wrong or justice, it was about positions and social status and as far as the idiot Nabal could see, David did not have a fine palace or fine clothes but was a fugitive in the wilderness. The reason for that did not matter to Nabal in his dog eat dog world and values.

"Every dog is rising against his master these days," he sneered in abuse of David.

David's men returned with the news of what Nabal had said and done and David was so angry he was prepared to kill the man there and then. The ridiculous thing is that if David and his men had just ridden in to take whatever provisions they wanted, Nabal could not have stopped them. To Nabal, poor meant insignificant and powerless. Period.

Like the obnoxious fool that he was, he did not even realise that he had cooked his own goose. Even his servants realised that his behaviour would result in problems with David and his men but he thought himself invincible and so looked down on everyone else. He did not even see that they, trained soldiers and vagabonds who had rallied under David could harm him. His servants took the trouble to go and tell Abigail because they knew that they would get some sense out of her.

This is really a very bad situation when the servants and the workers know what is going on and the wife has no idea. That is clearly trouble here. A good home is one in which the husband and wife communicate and know what they are doing together as a family. Abigail did not even know that David's men had been. She had to hear it from third parties. It says much for her that even when her own husband despised her so much, others did not. Her servants still held her in high regard and it is clear what the reason was for this from her reaction to these events.

Despite being so badly used by this so called husband, she cared for him or at least for her duties before God as a wife and mother of the household, not as a door mat but as a true worshipper of God. She still had agape love for Nabal even if eros had long and cleanly flown out of the window of that marriage as Nabal piled foolishness unto cruelty. With that agape love she prayed for him and took action to ensure that he was safe. When Abigail went to meet David to plead with him to spare her husband's household, she was not pleading for herself. Nothing would have happened to her when David and his men came on a revenge attack. She would have been safe but Nabal and his men and the males of his family would have been dead and she was not going to stand back and watch that happen. This is an act of great honour because it would have been so easy to just stand by. But then she was an honourable and good woman.

When she came back from going to plead for him before David, Nabal was having one of his banquets. She did not know about this either, her husband told her nothing. So she waited to speak to him.

Nabal did his usual act of drinking and debauchery and groping the serving wenches. But God had had enough. This obscene man ended up "brown bread." No one killed him. Not his wife, not David, not his faithful servants. Jehovah did.

If you are a battered wife, understand this very clearly. What is happening to you is very wrong. It is not just the secular world that is concerned about it. God almighty is always concerned about such things and in the days when there were no social services or injunction provisions, God had to step in to end the suffering of a lovely woman like yourself. God killed Nabal and he died. Because what Nabal was doing in the sight of God was an abomination.

That was not all God did for Abigail. Abigail became David's wife. To be married to a man like Nabal and end up with a man like David must be so euphoric that Abigail must have had to pinch herself many times. She must have been a very happy woman in the end. So you too can be one day if this relates to you. As you pray and keep yourself above reproach, God will surely undertake for you. I do not say he will kill your husband. That was a drastic step taken in circumstances where there were no real alternatives for the deliverance of this woman. But the Lord will certainly do what it takes to set you free and bring you into the longed for happiness that he intended for your life.

In some cases seeking the help of a Solicitor to

obtain an injunction may be a step that needs to be taken. In some cases, leaving the marriage may be necessary to avoid anyone losing their lives. Some women have been driven to murder their abusive husbands thus destroying further their own lives and that of their children. Some women have not taken action and been killed. Being prayerful and godly does not mean being stupid. Keep your brains and wits about you. Being in an abusive relationship is stupid and seeking for a solution within the marriage does not mean that you should be blind to wisdom. If a man is that violent, get out and seek solutions from outside the marriage whether it be to divorce or to try and solve the problem. God can solve any problem but remember, be wise.

# NEW TESTAMENT GIRLS

## MARY THE MOTHER OF THE LORD

*Piping down the valleys wild*
*Piping songs of pleasant glee*
*On a cloud I saw a child*
*And he laughing said to me*

*Pipe a song about a lamb*
*So I piped with merry cheer*
*Piper pipe that song again*
*So I piped he wept to hear*

*Piper sit thee down and write*
*In a book, that all may read*
*So he vanished from my sight*
*And I plucked a hollow reed,*

*And I made a rural pen,*
*And I stained the water clear*
*And I wrote my happy songs*
*Every child may joy to hear.*

William Blake

# The gospels

I am not a Catholic but I can well understand the awesome mystery of this particular woman, whose womb bore Jesus. She was just a simple, very young girl when the Angel told her that she would have a son and call his name Jesus for he as the lamb of God will deliver his people from all their sins. She had just become engaged and in those days to have a child out of wedlock was worse than murder or any other sin. Yet young Mary agreed without any question to do this. The reason must be her total lifelong obedience to Jehovah God. Her trust was without question. God would never ask her to do anything that was for her destruction. She trusted him completely and obeyed him completely. That was what made a simple, young girl of no great significance the Mother of the Lord Jesus and a vessel for the redemption of the world. You cannot be greater than that. Some were Judges, others Queens, prophets, architects and warriors but with a heart of total obedience, Mary topped them all. Not that anyone is competing but it is worth noting. Her portion was the greatest of the greats.

When the Angel informed Mary of what God wanted from her, there was not even a moment's hesitation about this. She asked obvious questions but immediately accepted the miraculous event prophesied. She did not doubt that she had an angelic visitation either. The Lord having let Joseph in on the mystery kept the family together.

Whether Mary had other children or not, is irrelevant to me. The Bible does refer to Jesus' brothers and sisters. It is no sin to have children in marriage.

The command to have children and multiply was given before the fall (Genesis 1:28). It formed no part of the disobedience of the fall. It was rather our hubris that we could discern as well as God and decide for ourselves what was good and what was not in opposition to the will of God, as in present day society, that was the great evil, rather than the choice of perfect obedience which God required from us for the perfect working of the universe. If it is your belief that Mary had no other children after Jesus and that she was herself the immaculate conception, that is up to you. I have no wish to argue for or against this. Mary was indeed awesome whatever the details.

Shortly after the mention of Jesus in the Temple around the period of his twelfth birthday, there was no further mention of Joseph. Mary must therefore have been a one parent family for quite a long time after Joseph died. This means that Jesus was brought up both in a loving family with two parents and also in a one parent family when he was still a very young man as it would appear that Joseph died. Yet he grew in the knowledge of God, he was faithful to the Ministry given to him and he did not once let his Father God down. All those who have been through any kind of family must remember that the Lord understands everything. It could also be said that he was a step-brother to his siblings for those who believe he had siblings and would understand that too. Their family worked perfectly because of the love of Mary, her understanding of who Jesus was and her total devotion to God. There is no greater role model for your children than God the Father, although the Lord also provides people who are good and proper influences in our lives when needed. He never leaves us desolate.

Mary was aware of the scriptures and as always bore revelation at the forefront of her mind. Very often the Bible said that Mary pondered events and statements in her mind. Whilst others did not understand, she understood from the first that her child was no ordinary person. She knew the facts. She had the revelation. In most spiritual things we too need revelation because it is experience that best counters the lies of the enemy. Yes we can argue about God and the things of the spirit but when we have had personal revelation, there are no further arguments. That is why the Lord says that unless we are born again spiritually and experience that revelation of truth, we cannot really know him.

When Jesus was born, Mary and Joseph took him as a baby into the temple to observe the Jewish rituals for the birth of a male child. The baby Jesus was presented to a well known temple prophet and rabbi named Simeon, who was of very advanced age and known to be waiting for the birth of the Messiah. But Mary and Joseph did not just show respect to the elderly man only. They showed that they honoured and recognised that women could be just as important as men spiritually because they sought out and also found Anna the prophetess, also of very great age and also waiting for the birth of the special child. In this they showed equal respect to the male and to the female. How could it be any other way? Those who have had themselves deep spiritual experience, have no trouble at all recognising this because they instinctively know the very heart of God for all people.

Mary was a good mother and did not suffer from the possessiveness of mothers. But she seems to have gone a little too far in not checking on the twelve year old Jesus when they went to the Temple in Jerusalem as a family. At twelve her son was still a child and having been introduced to the Temple for the first time was completely enthralled by it all. Mary must have been very good at teaching him the scriptures as was his earthly father Joseph because he had knowledge even then that astounded the rabbis and teachers. It cost them a day's journey but they found the Lord alive and well and discussing with the elders of the Temple. This little mishap is a comfort to every harassed mother with more than enough to do at all times. The Lord understands. His family went through it too. Even Mary could not do the motherhood thing perfectly all the time. Well does Luke say of little children that in heaven their (guardian) angels always behold our father's face. It should be a comfort to every Mum to know that God is watching over those children too, with the aid of his celestial hosts.

Mary did not interfere when the wedding couple ran out of wine in John 2. She must have been embarrassed for her poor relation who could not really afford that much and she knew that Jesus could help but she did not force the issue because she fully understood that Jesus would know what was best to be done. How many of us would have prevailed on our son in those circumstances with our rights as mothers to influence. Mary simply said to the disciples "Do whatever he asks you to do." She left him free to fulfil his ministry as led by his heavenly Father not as led by his earthly mother.

When it came to dying, she freely gave in to her son dying for you and for me. A small attempt to bring him home when the danger seemed to be mounting was only half- heartedly made but it is clear she was never serious about wanting him to come home because from the first she had understood that Jesus had a special mission on earth. That which she did not understand she was always willing to entrust to the Lord.

Mary watched her son die an excruciatingly painful death but she did not once desert him and remained at the foot of the cross. The bond between Mary and her son was clear and real. Even in the midst of pain, he did not forget her but made provisions for St John the Divine to care for his mother, which John faithfully did taking her, as Church history has it, to live with him in Ephesus. Mary must have been very charitable herself, allowing her son to be totally free with friends and followers and those who came to him for help. She shared him with the world because she knew in obedience to her heavenly Father that he belonged to the world. Her charity and hospitality was rewarded by John who looked after her thereafter.

Mary was in the upper room when the Holy Spirit came. Her understanding of who her son is, was very real indeed. She knew that it was not ending in disaster and loss. She knew that he was born to save the people from all their sins even as the angel told her.

Obedience is the most important quality that God wants from us. Obedience is the natural concomitant of love. If we love God enough, we will trust him in everything. We do not need to insist on our own right to decide because then we are saying that we know more than he does and we can think about what he has said and decide for ourselves. In one sense we do have that right and have always had that right. God in his love has given us the right to decide, but that we decide to obey him out of love and trust is what he truly desires. If we choose outside of his will, we have clearly chosen wrongly because God is perfect and by definition cannot make mistakes. The reality is that it was the disobedience of Adam our first human father that brought the power of Satan into the world. Satan himself, once a great Archangel in heaven also fell through disobedience. The reality of our relationship with God is that only those who have perfected their obedience to God will make it into his heaven. Those who have not cannot do so because then the whole spiral will start again with a rebellion in heaven itself, banishment and eons of the salvation process. God is not going to allow creation through all the events from Adam to Revelation a second time. We must understand the importance of perfecting our obedience and walking in the will of God with all our hearts. Otherwise, we will never make it. We plead the blood of Jesus, it is true, but we must remember that coming into the fellowship of those covered by the blood of the Son of God means acquiring the character of the Son of God. The essence of that character was perfect obedience to the will of the Father.

Many people ask questions about suffering and I believe that one of the answers is that God allows suffering in order to perfect our obedience. When you have got to that place where no matter what is going on, you know he loves you and is in control and able to deal with the situation, however long it takes, whatever form it takes, then you know you are finally beginning your life journey as a true disciple of Jesus Christ. For the fair-weather Christians who preach that you become a millionaire and nothing bad ever happens to you, good luck to them. But I have not found such promises in my Bible. What I have found is that whether times are good or bad, the Lord is with those who believe and trust in him. Whether in famine or plenty, the Lord will provide for those who trust in him and live in obedience to his will.

# MARY MAGDALENE

*Teach us good Lord, to serve thee as thou deservest*
*To give and not to count the cost*
*To fight and not to heed the wounds*
*To toil and not to seek for rest*
*To labour and not to ask for any reward*
*Save that of knowing that we do thy will*

Prayer of Ignatius Loyola Founder of the Jesuits
Believed to have been originally prayed by
Mary Magdalene

## The Gospels

Strangely enough she was not a prostitute as often said. No one quite has any idea how it came about that she was called this. Mary of Magdalene had seven demons cast out of her. She was identified with the name of the city that she came from and she was one of the ladies like Susanna the wife of Chuza Herod's Steward who looked after the Lord financially so she must have been wealthy and from a prominent family in Magdala, a merchant city.

She like all who followed him was devoted to him and never once deserted him even in his hour of death, even when others did. She was at the foot of the Cross with Jesus as was his mother and Mary of Bethany and many of the women. All the Apostles except John who was quite young had run away. The women were not in as much danger as the men to be fair because with

Jesus having been arrested and crucified, his followers could have been picked up any time. However we cannot under-estimate what these women did and the courage they showed when it all seemed to go sour. How their hearts must have bled to watch their beloved Son, Rabbi and friend who had never harmed anybody hanging there on the cross on some trumped up charges! Sometimes we put our own pain before the pain of others who we love and who are suffering but not these women. They ensured they were there for the Lord, however much their hearts broke.

Mary of Bethany had anointed the Lord for his burial. Mary of Magdala went alone and fearless to anoint his body further for burial. Although Joseph of Arimathea took his body to be buried in the tomb, Mary wanted to make absolutely sure that his body had all the final rituals and preparations made. Nothing was too much trouble for her Lord.

Jerusalem must have been a very fearful and dangerous time in that period. Having just completed this public crucifixion, nature itself had turned against the land. There had been an earthquake, reports were made that some who had died some time before were being spotted in the city; the veil of the Temple had been torn in two, the Jewish rabble who shouted for the crucifixion of the Lord must have been wandering the streets drunk with the orgy of blood-lust and the Roman soldiers must have been very confused not knowing what was right or who was right. A confused soldier can be a very dangerous person because out of fear and insecurity they could kill anyone. Kill first and questions afterwards they may think in their fear and insecurity.

In this atmosphere, Mary went alone to look for the body of the Lord, to ensure that he had been properly anointed and prepared for his burial. She was in grave danger, no doubt about that, but she did not care. Jesus came first, dead or alive.

I would like to think that Mary was expecting the resurrection, that she above all understood some of the things the Lord had said before his crucifixion but that cannot be read into the biblical passages. She was as ignorant as the rest of the disciples and Apostles of the meaning of many things that Jesus said until after his resurrection when he explained things to them in full, in the forty days before his ascension. She went to the grave out of love to do the last thing she could ever do for the Lord. Those who have lost dear close ones will understand this, the need to ensure that they have the best preparation for being laid to rest. It is the last act of love and it is of great importance for those who have been touched by it.

But Jesus was not dead, he was but he had conquered death and risen again. It was not possible that death could have dominion over him because he was without sin. It was not possible that the grave could hold him because he has all authority in heaven and on earth. In his crucifixion the devil scored the greatest own goal of all time. Jesus had conquered death and had risen from the grave!

Mary did not understand in fact. When she could not find his body, she only wept. When the Lord himself came to her in the very early hours of the morning just as dawn was breaking, she did not recognise him. How could she? In her mind set at the time, he was dead. How like many of us who do not recognise him in our darkest moments and yet he is there. Did the Pslamist David not say "Though I walk through the valley of the shadow of death, thou art with me." In Revelation 2:17 we are told that Jesus also has a special name for each of us who overcomes. The Lord has a special name which will be only known to him and to us. One day the Lord will call those of us who make it by our special name that he has reserved over eons of time for us. I can hardly wait. Then we will say with faces shining with love "Rabboni" which means my Master / Teacher.

It was not until the Lord called her name in that special way that he used to, that she realised it was Jesus. Now many of us would have then run for our lives from this ghost, but Mary was fearless. Love made her fearless, till she understood that she was not talking to a ghost but to the risen Lord.

"Go and tell your brethren that I am risen." The Lord asked her.

In these simple words we can sum up something of what Jesus thought of women in those days and what he thinks of us now.

In those days, despite all that God had done through women in the Old Testament, there had elapsed some four hundred years since the prophet Malachi in which there had been no prophets of the calibre of those in the Old Testament until John the Baptist. In this period in which there was a paucity of the presence of the Spirit of God, the oppression against women increased. The oppression of women tends to proliferate where there is no real light and by the time Jesus was born, little Jewish boys were taught to pray every morning,

"Lord, I thank you that I am not a gentile, a slave or a woman."

Women could not give valid evidence in a Court of law and indeed when the Temple was rebuilt, it was built with the Court of Women, whereas the Temple of Solomon did not have such a demarcation.

Jesus cut through all this disrespect and disregard of women. In the first place he had women followers. Many who have argued against the ordination of women have often said that Jesus did not have women as disciples. Neither did he have gentile men. All his disciples were Jewish men. It would have been entirely inappropriate to have women with them all the time in those days, but to the extent that it was possible, there were in fact women who sometimes travelled with them when appropriate but mostly they played the role of financing their work and financing their rest times or hosting them when they were preaching in their area.

Despite all this cultural and legal prejudice against women in his day, Jesus chose a woman as the first witness of the resurrection.

"Why?" I once asked the Lord

"Because she was there," he said.

It is important that we understand that although God has a blueprint for the life of everyone of us, there are many things that are up to us and to those who love much, much will be given, to those who give much, much will be given, to those who persevere most, success will be given and so on. God has created us and given us free will. We play as much a part in what happens to us within his will as he does. It is a two way street. We must always remember that. If we cleanse and prepare ourselves for noble use, God will honour that.

"Of a truth," Peter said "God is no respecter of persons, but in every age and every nation, anyone who does his will is acceptable to him."

Jesus does not care for our man made rules as to who is a second class citizen and who is a nobody. To him anyone who comes to him is acceptable to him. What matters to him is the heart. It is love and joy and peace and the kindness and goodness of our hearts that count when we walk with him, not our sex, our race or our worldly standing or wealth.

Most of the teachings of Jesus in the Temple appear to be in the Court of Women for the simple reason that the women could not go into the Court of men and he always wanted the women to hear what he had to say as much as the men.

He also demonstrated what he thought of some of the religious rules of the Pharisees and Sadducees that had grown into Jewish religious traditions. A woman who had a period was considered unclean. Whilst this rule may initially have started as hygiene issues it developed into something else and by the time of Jesus anyone who even sat near a woman who was bleeding as a result of her period or for whatever reason had become ritually unclean and had to go through all types of cleansing procedure before being considered clean again.

One day as Jesus was on his way to the home of Jairus the ruler of the synagogue, a woman with an issue of blood, who had bled for twelve years because of some medical problem, approached him. She was too ashamed to ask openly for healing. She probably thought Jesus would not touch her. But she thought, bless her, that if she could but touch the hem of his garment, she would be made whole. She stole up to the Lord even in that great crowd and touched him. Power came from the garment of Jesus and healed her.

"Who touched me?" said Jesus.

I rather think the all seeing and all knowing Lord knew very well who had touched him. But he wanted to make an important point. He wanted her to come forward. He wanted her to stop being ashamed as she had nothing to be ashamed of. He wanted her to know that she might have been sick but that did not mean she was dirty. He wanted her and everyone to know that their requirement of ritual uncleanness in these circumstances were not to his liking or approval.

Having made her healing public, Jesus then went from having been touched by this woman directly into the home of Jairus, to heal Jairus' child. He did not undergo any rituals for cleansing for having been touched by this woman. The leader of the synagogue who would have been one of those seriously enforcing these oppressive and demeaning rules allowed Jesus in his house. There was no talk about ritual uncleanness. How could there be? His need was greater than his rules. His daughter was more important than a form which he knew in his heart meant nothing. No one stopped Jesus going into the home of Jairus that day. The Lord had made clear where he stood with regard to oppressive, meaningless rules that undermined a class of people for no good reason.

Of Mary Magdalene, there is really little else to say as the Bible does not really give her that much prominence. She was the first witness of the resurrection because she loved enough to be at the right place at the right time. She was in the upper room on the day of Pentecost and remained an important part of the early Church playing very much the role she had always played and assisting whenever she could. Her devotion to the Lord remains clear and the prayer attributed to Mary Magdalene by the early church says it all.

The claims of Daniel Brown in the Da Vinci Code is part of the plot of the enemy to derail Christianity in these end times. It is part of the conspiracy against Christianity in the so called dawning of the age of Aquarius. But the impact of these claims has proved negligible.

Purely and simply Jesus cannot have another bride because a bride has already been chosen for him, that is the Church and secondly, Jesus cannot have a special blood-line because we are all his special blood-line. Those who write such things have simply failed to understand the significance of the coming of Christ. He came to die, to shed his perfect blood in payment for our sinful life. He came to make a contractual exchange. If the wages of sin is death and the sinless dies in place of the sinner, then the debt is paid for the sinful who can then live in place of the sinless. This contract would operate for whosoever accepts the exchange. All the theories of marriage and special heirs are just madness and evil. His bride is the Church and his heirs are the Church.

# A WOMAN OF THE CITY
# AND MARY OF BETHANY

*And it came to pass, as Jesus sat at meat in the house,*
*Behold, many publicans and sinners came and sat down*
*with him and his disciples.*
*And when the Pharisees saw this they said unto his*
*disciples*
*"Why eateth your Master with publicans and sinners?"*
*But when Jesus heard this, he said unto them*
*"Those that are whole do not need a physician but those*
*that are sick*
*I am not come to call the righteous, but sinners to*
*repentance."*

Matthew 9:11-12

## The Gospels

In the book of Matthew the genealogist of Christ stops to acknowledge unusually two female ancestors. One was Ruth the foreigner and immigrant and the other was Rahab the prostitute. Some of the accusations against Christ were that he spent time with sinners, prostitutes and the hated tax collectors as well as many others against who society turned up its nose for whatever reason. His reason was given quite clearly in the above passage.

The Lord teaches further that it is not what a person eats for instance that pollutes him, it is not outward things or rituals, it is the state of the heart and out of the abundance of the heart, the mouth speaks.

What we do is governed by what is in our hearts and a person whose heart has been cleansed by the power of the Holy Spirit can no longer be judged by their past. It is not how you started that counts, it is how you finish.

In the gospels, there is a story of the woman of the city who anointed Jesus' feet with very expensive alabaster oil and wiped his feet with her hair. She was a prostitute and the anointing with such oil shows that this woman despite her sordid past recognised the kingship and greatness of Jesus. In his presence she knew only tears of repentance for her sins and honour of him as King. Did she know that she too was anointing him for his burial? Did she know that he was the Messiah? There is no indication of that but there is little doubt that there was a woman who knew. She too in a separate incident anointed the feet of Jesus with the most expensive oil there was for his burial. She knew who he was.

Mary of Bethany was the sister of Martha and Lazarus. She was a friend of Jesus together with her sister Mary and her brother Lazarus whom the Lord had raised from the dead. When Jesus taught, she sat at his feet with the men and listened. Burning stews and unpolished furniture meant nothing to her at those times. Listening to the word of God was sweeter and more important than anything else. When her sister Martha rebuked her for not bothering with the housework, Jesus made it clear that seeking the word of God was more important than preparing for the Lord's comfort. Nothing is more important than the word of God. His word is life and will never return to him empty until it has accomplished that for which he sent it forth. His word is power, he speaks and it is done. His word is a lamp unto our feet. How can a young man keep his way pure? By guarding them in accordance with your word. Lord I have stored your word in my heart that I may not sin against thee (Extracts from Psalm 119).

The resurrection of Lazarus was a landmark. Suddenly this teacher, rabbi who healed the sick and made everyone feel so good about themselves raised a man who had been in the tomb four days. Mary and Martha and all those present were blown away but for Mary it was quite a bit more. I believe that she alone along with Peter in his confession at Caesaria- Philippi, of his disciples, realised that Jesus is the Christ, before he went to the Cross and rose again. After his resurrection he told them everything but it is remarkable that this young lady knew not only that Jesus was the Messiah but that he was going to be crucified. There is little doubt that she knew because when she anointed him with oil and washed his feet with her tears, the Lord made it clear that she was doing the right thing and was anointing him for his burial. How did she know? Well she simply paid attention. Secondly her love for the Saviour knew no bounds. Most importantly she knew that only the Christ could have raised her brother. As I have said before, experiencing the power of God removes many questions coming from doubt and those who have experienced it know that it is the greatest miracle of all.

# ST PAUL A MISOGYNIST?

*I have fought the good fight*
*I have finished my course*
*I have kept the faith*
*Henceforth there is laid up for me*
*A crown of righteousness,*
*Which the Lord, the righteous Judge,*
*Shall give me at that day.*
St Paul of Tarsus (2 Timothy 4:6-7)

I have heard it said that the great Apostle and Saint, Paul of Tarsus, was a misogynist but I do not know how anyone could say such a thing. St Paul clearly worked with women. Aquilla and Priscilla, a husband and wife team, were not only Apostles who worked with Paul but he shared the hand-craft of tent-making with them. Euodia and Synticke worked with him and even though they fell out, he simply urged them to put aside their differences recalling perhaps when he himself had fallen out with his friend Barnabbas. He knew Eunice Timothy's grandmother and his mother and showed great respect for any number of women. He sent greetings to Nympha and the Church in her house and in Romans 16 he sends greetings to Junia who was an Apostle before him. In those days that particular name could belong to a man or a woman and there are many who believe that the particular Apostle in question was a woman.

Paul was the first Apostle to preach in Europe. In a dream he had seen a man saying,

"Come over to Macedonia and help us."

He realised then that the Lord was asking him to go into Europe. When he arrived, the first people he met and who received him were a group of businesswomen who met at the great business mall, Lydia and her friends. Through their positive reception, the gospel got into Europe from where it went to all corners of the earth.

Paul uttered one of the most clear equality and diversity statements in scripture. In his letter to the Galatians he said

"There is neither Jew nor Greek, there is neither bond nor free, there is neither male nor female, for ye are all one in Christ."

Galatians 3:28

Yet Paul did say to the Corinthian Church that a woman is not to speak or teach in Church. I rather think that was an issue specific to the Corinthian Church and many others like them. It is clear that there was a problem with noise as far as the Corinthian Church was concerned. It is likely that men and women sat separately and sometimes the wives would shout questions across the room at their husbands. They would answer. The result was mayhem and I do not think that anyone would disagree that is not appropriate for a Church service. Everything rather should be done in order and if people have questions of their partners, they could ask them at home.

St Peter and the other Apostles, as St Paul made clear, travelled with their wives. Paul was never married but for him marriage was just a luxury that he did not allow himself as he was so busy with the gospel. Some people are called to be eunuchs or make themselves eunuchs for the sake of the kingdom of God.

St Peter spoke very kindly about women and about marriage. He commands husbands to love their wives, bestowing honour on the woman as the weaker sex, not the inferior sex. We are physically weaker than men but spiritually and emotionally are if anything stronger. God had his ways of creating balance between us. He refers to the woman as joint heir with the man of the grace of life. One way a man can ensure that his prayers are not answered is by being mean to his wife, according to Peter. The man is said to be the head of the woman. Not all men are head of women but in a relationship, a man may have that headship in the same way as God the father is said to be the head of Christ. This headship does not imply inequality. Each family should work out how this operates for them but I reckon that Deborah and the Shunemite and the Virtuous woman had it just right. With each one their husband had prominence even when they themselves also had prominence. That is just the way that it is. For many the edge of leadership will be the man's. Where the edge is forced to be the woman's either because her husband is weak or they do not understand this spiritual way of relating, there is no real happiness. I do not know why it is so but it just is. One of the reasons why there are so many divorces today amongst younger women is their lack of understanding of this spiritual order of things. They must work things out so that there is a leadership in the man which does not imply inferiority in the woman or suffocate her abilities, initiatives and action. How each person works it out may be a little different to another but work it out they must in order to reach real stability and happiness. A man needs to know that he is valued and respected by his wife and it does no harm at all to tell him so.

# IN THE BEGINNING

*Of man's first disobedience, and the fruit*
*Of that forbidden tree, whose mortal taste*
*Brought death into the world and all our woe*
*With loss of Eden till one greater man*
*Restore us, and regain the blissful seat,*
*Sing, heavenly muse, that on the secret tops*
*Of Horeb, or of Sinai, didst inspire*
*That shepherd, who first taught the chosen seed,*
*In the beginning how the heavens and earth*
*Rose out of chaos: Or if Sion Hill*
*Delight thee more and Siloa's brook that flowed*
*Past by the Oracle of God; I thence*
*Invoke thy aid to my adventurous Song.....*

*And chiefly thou O Spirit, that dost prefer*
*Before all Temples the upright heart and pure*
*Instruct me, for Thou know'st: Thou from the first*
*Wast present, and with mighty wings outspread*
*Dove-like satst brooding on the vast Abyss*
*And mad'st it pregnant: What in me is dark*
*Illumine, what is low raise and support;*
*That to the height of this great Argument*
*I may assert th'Eternal Providence,*
*And justifie the ways of God to men.*

*Say first, for heaven hides nothing from thy view*
*Nor the deep trace to hell, say first what cause*
*Moved our grand parents in that happy state*
*Favoured of heaven so highly to fall off*
*From their Creator and transgress his will*

*For one restraint, Lord of the World besides?*
*Who first seduced them to that foul revolt*
John Milton *Paradise Lost*


## Genesis 1 – 3

Begin at the beginning, the March Hare said. Clearly the most sensible place to begin but I have not done that for good reason. The beginning is the creation story of Adam and Eve and the story of the fall of man and I did not want those who do not believe in the creation story to miss the truths contained in this book, which is that women are as important to God as men and God can use any of us to sublime, grandiose and epic levels. But whether you believe in the creation story or not, the reality is that without it you cannot really understand the rest of the good book. You can pick and choose from the Bible but that is the very thing the fall of man was about. It was about our desire to have the right to decide against God's orders and counsel rather than to obey God. We do indeed have the right to decide, but we simply have to understand what the consequences are. If, having the right to decide, we had any sense, we would understand one thing, that God is omniscient, omnipotent and omnipresent and if this is true, how can we know better than he does? Therefore it should be enough for us that he said "Thou shalt not...."

God created man for fellowship with him and when God finished creating in the perfect garden, Eden, he looked over his creation and we are told it was very good. However there was one thing which

God saw and said was not good. The man was alone. It was God himself who said "It is not good that man shall be alone." So he put the man to sleep and brought out from a very major bone in his side, the woman. She was already there inside the man. Everything had already been created. We are told that God made them both in his own image. There is a clear picture of equality in Genesis 1:27-28 in the first reference to the creation of man and woman.

But over the years we are told that men began to interpret this passage as meaning that Adam had a first wife. They even gave a name for her. They call her Lilith and hold her responsible for bringing evil into the world. They say Lilith was evil because she considered herself equal to Adam. They point to Chapter 2 of Genesis in reference to Chapter 1 as a new story. This is monstrous and shows to what extent people will go to deny the equality of women. Chapter 2 of Genesis is simply a fuller explanation of Chapter 1. There is absolutely nothing to suggest there was a second wife for Adam. Those who believe such things have been influenced by the same sources as the legends of Pandora in Greek mythology. From time immemorial men have denied the equality of women and there is a reason for this. The reason for this lies in the Genesis account itself. In Genesis Chapter 3 in addition to the story of the fall of man, there is a promise of the redemption of man. A woman born of woman shall bear a child who will destroy the devil. The devil understood this threat from the beginning. What he did not know was the plan of God. He did not know what time, what race, what woman was going to bear this child and so from the beginning THE

WOMAN became an enemy of the devil. Our menfolk were incited against us. Wherever a woman is denied her rights, wherever a woman is hit and oppressed, wherever a woman is not allowed to follow her God given dream, it is the devil at work, operating the same old hatred that entered into his heart against the woman right there in the garden of Eden. God in return gave woman special discerning gifts that would enable her to cope even without great physical strength.

Was Eve responsible for all the evil of the world? If Eve had not accepted the apple from Satan and given some to Adam, we would all have been saved a lot of grief and suffering and we would all have lived in perfect Eden. The whole earth would eventually have been made as perfect as Eden as we went forth and multiplied over the face of the earth. I have always been taught that it was Eve who did this, just as Pandora or Lilith did. Whatever name she had, it was her fault. Even John Milton in his great epic "Paradise Lost" puts the major blame on Eve.

I decided to read my Bible for myself and I found out that when God had given the command to Adam to beware of the tree of knowledge of good and evil, Eve had not been brought out of him yet. She had not yet been born. So if Adam never told her what God told them, how was she to know?

I believe that Eve did not in fact know for certain that she was not to eat of the fruit of that tree. She had seen Adam avoid the tree. But there is no record that Adam had ever bothered to tell her about the tree to be avoided. Let us learn from this. A marriage without proper communication is a marriage in trouble.

Anything can go wrong. Adam was wrong not to tell his wife everything about their life together and Eve was wrong not to ask. She was made as a partner to the man not as a child or second class citizen. In reality many men are not good at communication but a good wife can gradually bring them without nagging to communicate. It is also worth noting here that men are different from women however equal we are. Throw a ball to a male child and he will kick it but the female child will catch it as a rule. These differences go back to the cradle. We have different hormones and we have different styles of doing things. Sometimes we have different brain patterns especially in the area of emotions rather than intellect. A woman, because of child bearing, has a greater nesting instinct than a man and the ability to create a home although many men when they understand or have ability in this area, can be excellent. With patience and understanding and communication we can build the strength of our partners in areas in which they are not very good but which are vital to our marriage or relationship when you are courting, and indeed during the life of the marriage.

When Eve was told by the devil to eat the fruit of the tree, she asked questions which show that she really was unsure what the situation was.

"Did God say we should not eat this?"

She wanted to know. The devil lied to her of course. Ignorance is a dangerous thing. We should always take the trouble to keep ourselves informed through newspapers, books and other sources of national news of the things going on in our communities and in our lives too. If you and your husband are close enough and you are alert to what he is doing including at work, you may be able to spot that secretary or colleague who is bent on taking him away and you may be able to alert him and put a stop to things before he gets in too deep to get out. If your children are having problems at school, keep yourself informed as to the reasons why. You may be able to understand those reasons and when you understand the cause, you will have a better idea of the solution. One of the reasons why I love the Shunemite so much is that she was able to saddle her horse and go and find the prophet who would pray and her son would come back to life. She did not have to wait till her husband came home. She was not so dependent on him that she was of no earthly use to him, as some women can be, thinking that they are being obedient and putting their husbands first. You are a partner not a maid or a child or a servant or a dependent.

I believe that Eve ate that apple because she did not know for sure that God had ordered them not to but Adam knew for sure. Yet it is Eve that is blamed by men and women down the ages for the fall of man. They were both at fault because Eve should have found out for sure instead of playing the "dumb blonde". But it was Adam who knowing clearly and squarely that he was disobeying Jehovah, took the apple and ate it.

What gets me about the constant blame of the woman in this story is that the rest of the Bible places the responsibility clearly and squarely on Adam but that does not stop the Christian Church and men and women all over the world blaming Eve. Romans 5:14 refers to Adam's transgression.

"Wherefore, as by one man sin entered into the world, and death by sin, so death passed upon all men, for all have sinned.......For if through the offence of one, many be dead, much more the grace of God and the gift by grace, which is by one man, Jesus Christ hath abounded unto many."

Romans 5:12-15

When God came into the garden to deal with our miscreant parents, he called to Adam. Some say at this time they were both called Adam because it was only in Chapter 4 that the woman was ever referred to as Eve. Perhaps she was Eve all the time. Perhaps she was Adam before that. It does not matter. God gave the responsibility for the sin to Adam whether it be the man alone or the man and the woman together. Whichever way it was, the responsibility or the greater responsibility belonged to Adam.

Yet it is Eve that has been blamed all down the ages. In many Churches preachers and blamers have gone on to tie up Eve with Delilah, the wife of Samson who deceived him and Jezebel the wife of King Ahab, who was allowed by the King to take control of his country and bring in the worship of idols. She was an immoral and evil woman, a plotter of murders and intrigues and a destroyer of the people of God. They go on to preach that women tempt men to do evil and are to be put down and avoided at all costs and treated as objects of temptation and evil. Marry them so that you can have a source for sex, children and housekeeping but do not let the woman into your heart or allow her to fulfil her own life. There is the fear that if she is given or allowed authority, she will somehow morph into a Jezebel. This is disgusting. These women Delilah, Jezebel, Vashti and Herodias are not Christian women. They are pagan worshippers and idolators. How could they be role models for any decent woman?

So why is it that women have been so oppressed and mislabelled down the ages? The answer lies in Genesis itself. God created a perfect Eden so why did he have to go and create the tree of knowledge of good and evil that we were not to eat. Simply this. True love involves free choice. God did not make robots. He gave each of his created beings the right to decide for himself. Love is not fully love when it has not chosen to love. God wanted us to choose him, out of love. The tree was the test of choice, the test of trust. In obedience we are stating that Father knows best, not that we know as much as he, God, does. Well, we did not choose Jehovah God, we disobeyed and listened to Satan.

Satan is also a created being. He was the most favoured of all the archangels. But pride entered his heart and he rebelled against Jehovah. Some say it is because of the creation of man and he was jealous and despised man. There was a war in heaven of which John Milton wrote so beautifully. Milton then goes on to write that the serpent deceived the mother of mankind. It is true that Eve was the first point of contact but I do not agree that she carries the major responsibility for the deception. Milton much as I love his poetry was however simply reflecting the common view of his time and of time immemorial. The woman was to blame in the garden. She was deceived and deceived the man and woman is responsible for the fall from Eden and the woes of life. Even in ancient mythology it was Pandora or Lilith who opened a box and released all the evil of the world.

With Satan, death and decay and suffering entered the world. Eden was removed until its time of restoration. But this destruction of God's creation was not a total surprise to him. God knows all things and cannot be taken by surprise. He had already seen the potential and had the antidote prepared. That antidote, the salvation of all creation from the ravages of disobedience was decided on before all things were created, before the foundation of the world was laid. Satan did not know it because he was a created being and the antidote in case it all went wrong had been decided by those who were not created but have been from all time, Father Son and Holy Spirit the three manifestations of God. Satan did not know it. Had he known it, he would not have killed the Lord of glory on the cross of Calvary scoring against himself, the greatest own goal of all time.

In Genesis 3:15, God had prophesied that a man born of woman shall destroy the devil. The seed was to be born. The devil had no idea when, which tribe, country or people his destroyer was to come from. And so from time immemorial, the woman became a special object of hatred for the devil. The devil was there egging man and woman on when they denied the right of the woman to achieve alongside the man, when the husband beat his wife, when the woman was not allowed to vote or to take high office in the land, when the woman was denied the right to spiritual things despite clear gifts. As far as the spiritual realm is concerned, the devil scores a double point in the old attitudes because not only does he upset and destroy his great enemy woman, but he also halves the army of God. How clever! And how stupid of the churchmen who allow him to do so, restricting what a woman can and cannot do in the Church despite obvious gifting by the Holy Spirit for such jobs. No, woman was to be destroyed and punished and kept from the limelight just out of sheer venom of the potential that she carried, to bear a child that would destroy the devil. Men in ignorance played along. Women in ignorance accepted defeat and agreed to their own mistreatment.

And at the appointed time, Mary of Nazareth, a descendant of the line of David, bore a child and called his name Jesus in accordance with the instructions of the Archangel Gabriel who had foretold his Royal birth as man.

"For God so loved the world that he gave his only begotten son that whosoever believes in him shall not perish but have everlasting life."
John 3:16

The death of Jesus meant the shedding of blood because under the eternal laws of Jehovah within which Satan and Eden fell, the wages of sin is death. Jesus died to pay the price for our sins. He was without sin and therefore death could not hold him and he rose again. This means that for whosoever accepts, the price of that person's sin is paid. It is a perfectly valid legal transaction. If you are in debt, someone can come along and pay that for you. That is what Jesus did. Therefore the free gift of God is eternal life in Christ

Jesus, because Jesus had paid the debt for sin which is death under eternal law.

It was this Easter at the time of writing that it struck me for the first time that Mary had found the risen Christ in the garden. Our destruction had started in a garden. Our redemption was completed in a garden. Echoes of Eden. How like Jehovah to give us that reminder to help us to understand until the time when he makes all things new.

Genesis 3:15 also makes an important statement. It says that God has put a special enmity between the devil and the woman. What a great responsibility that is for womankind.

My dear girls, do you understand that God has given you a special enmity against the devil? Do you understand that you have a special God-given discernment of the wiles of the devil. Do you understand that you have the spiritual power to deal with it all? Use it. Use it in prayer, in daily strength of character in making the right choices, in progress, in knowledge and awareness of the good and the dangers around you in every form and most of all in protecting your family and in protecting your country. It was Jael who refused to fraternize with the enemy even when her husband did and when the enemy made the mistake of running into her home, she destroyed him. It was the Shunemite who recognised the man of God and brought great blessing to her home by acknowledging the man of God and making provisions for him. There are things that you will spot before your husband does because of the powers God has given you. Many of us call it intuition.

Sarah the wife of Abraham is a woman who has

often been blamed for causing a catastrophe that will yet lead to the end of the world as we know it and has caused the turmoil of the Arab world politics. She did not wait for the word of God to be fulfilled concerning the birth of Isaac but thought she could assist God. She was a good woman and had an excellent marriage with her husband Abraham. It must have cost her dear to give him another woman to sleep with so that a child could be born to Abraham in accordance with the prophecy to him. But she forgot that the prophecy had been to herself also and made the mistake of thinking that she did not matter to God. Although she was being selfless, she was actually belittling herself and not trusting God.

The birth of Ishmael by her servant Hagar whom she gave to Abraham was a problem and remains a problem till this day, it was that huge. Yet when there was a crisis in the household and Sarah had asked Abraham to send Hagar and the child away, God said to Abraham "Listen to your wife." (Genesis 21:12)

God did not write Sarah off despite what was probably the hugest mistake of all time by a wife. Its consequences we still live with today. Men who equally listen to their wives often will find wisdom in what she has to say even if she is not perfect. We do see and we do have insight and it is a wise man who recognises that. If your husband does not recognise that, continue to pray that he will and as time goes by, he will see your wisdom for himself. Any demonic forces that attack you or your children or your family you have the power to destroy in prayer and through wise action. Many times situations will require action, not just the believer praying without any knowledge of what action they may have to take. But that action will always be scriptural so please check with your pastor or vicar or church friends. Jesus said

> "Behold I give you power to tread on serpents and scorpions, and over all the power of the enemy and nothing shall by any means hurt you."

Luke

10:19

Always pray in the Name of Jesus, the Name that is above all names. Always pray in reference to the blood of Jesus when you are dealing with demonic attacks. This is not the place to go into spiritual warfare strategies. You may find my book Prayer is the Master Key helpful.

Today the family is being minimised and decimated in many modern day civilisations. The reason for this is that the family is an institution given by God from the beginning, in Eden, where we can know something of the love of God. The family is a place for us to have love and security. With that love and security, we can go out into the world and be proper citizens, but the devil has deceived many politicians. They point at malfunctioning families and use them to judge and decry the family. They point to the fact that not all have wonderful families to say that it is wrong for some to have wonderful families because it is unfair. The devil continues to drive these upside down grundnorms born of the politics of envy and born of our desire to create a utopia on earth without God, an impossible task. This had been further re-enforced by the fall of communism in various previously communist regimes. First and last, this cannot be done. The government can shout till they are blue in the face that young people must go to University but until they have been nurtured into that knowledge, in the home, in their early days or even in their latter days, they cannot grasp it. Many continue to think that they can do better than the set down rules as shown in the Bible. Well they cannot and society continues to fall apart as we continue to seek a secular non-God world.

As I watch the immorality of women today, I blush for shame. Modern liberation movements for women have sought the rights to behaviour like men and have the same attitude as men. Well we have got it all now. We can now have as many one night stands as we want. We can now drink ourselves into the gutter anytime. We can wear clothes that make some of us wonder why we bother to wear any clothes at all and if any man so much as comes near, we can shout rape if we want and destroy that man forever. Yes we now have top jobs and we do what we like but the question is "are we happy with this?" I personally do not believe anybody can be really happy until they go God's way, live God's way. All the dos and don'ts of God's way are simply there to protect us. God is not a kill joy. He wants us to have real joy. He wants us to have things that have lasting meaning and satisfaction. A quick thrill from that gorgeous man who does not phone and does not return your calls and leaves you feeling like used toilet tissue is hardly worth it compared to that husband of more years that you care to remember who has always been there and who over the years has come to tick all the boxes. God wants the second one for you because he loves you and if you keep running around chasing cheap and quick thrills, you will never spot the real thing.

God understands our sexuality. He made it for goodness sake. But how many of us have been really happy after that one night stand and he never calls? Human beings are built to experience this wonderful relationship between a man and a woman in the safety of a permanent relationship which is marriage. And for those who think sex is evil, please note that the command to go forth and multiply was given before the fall not after the fall. This was not the sin of Eden. The sin of Eden was simply disobedience and is clearly stated to be so. Our redemption came with the God man who lived in perfect obedience. Jesus. God for our own good has commanded us to live in this way only in a secure and permanent relationship to avoid all the hurt and pain that anything else would cause us. Wise up and listen to him for he knows best. If you are honest with yourself, you know this already and if you give yourself a chance, you will see that it is true.

Girls, is it not time for us women in the nation to begin to change things? It is the devil who wants us to live in a broken society. Why not put aside the devil's agenda and go God's way, then you will be a blessing to your children, your husband and your nation. Pray for yourself, your family and your friends and for your nation. Learn from the Bible and the Church how to live a fulfilled and happy life. Give your heart to Jesus and in all your ways acknowledge him and he shall direct your path. Then you will blossom like the rose that you are. You will be like the Rose of Sharon.